MEDIA/SOCIAL

Course Book on
Sociology of Media and Society

MEDIA/SOCIAL

Course Book on
Sociology of Media and Society

R KUMARAN

**Xpress
Publishing**
Notion Press Media Pvt Ltd

Made with ♥ on the Notion Press Platform

www.notionpress.com

Published by
Xpress
Publishing
Notion Press Media Pvt Ltd,
Old No. 38, New No. 6, McNichols
Road, Chetpet, Chennai, Tamil
Nadu 600031

To Students who wanted this book

Table of Contents

Foreword 1

Preface 3

Acknowledgements 6

Introduction 8

MEDIA AND SOCIETY 13

KEY IDEAS IN MEDIA STUDIES 57

MEDIA AND SOCIAL STRUCTURE 101

MEDIA AND LAWS 121

MEDIA AND SOCIETY: PRACTICE 137

BIBLIOGRAPHY 167

Foreword

In an era defined by the relentless march of technology and the ever-expanding reach of media, it is imperative to critically examine the intricate relationship between media, culture, and society. This book, "Media/Social," serves as a compass to navigate the complex terrain where these three realms intersect, offering insights into how media shapes and is shaped by the cultural and social contexts in which it operates.

The book's exploration begins by tracing the historical trajectory of media, from the invention of the printing press to the rise of digital platforms. Each technological advancement has brought about profound shifts in how we communicate, access information, and perceive the world. The printing press democratized knowledge, the radio, United Nations and television brought visual storytelling into our homes, and the internet created a global village, connecting individuals across vast distances.

As we examine this historical evolution, we consider how each media era has shaped cultural production, social interactions, and power dynamics. By understanding the past, we gain insights into the present and can better anticipate the future of media and its impact on society.

The book delves into the theoretical frameworks that have shaped media studies to fully grasp the complex interplay between media, culture, and society. These frameworks provide the tools to analyse how media operates within specific cultural and social contexts, revealing the mechanisms through which it exerts influence.

We explore Marxist perspectives that critique media's role in perpetuating power dynamics and ideological control, highlighting how media ownership and content often serve the ruling class's interests. The Frankfurt School's critical theory further illuminates how the culture industry can promote conformity and consumerism, shaping public consciousness to inhibit critical thought.

The book also examines the work of Marshall McLuhan, whose assertion that "the medium is the message" challenges us to consider the profound effects of media technologies beyond their content. The rise of postmodernism invites us to question contemporary media culture's fragmented and hyperreal nature, where the lines between reality and representation blur.

The rapid advancements in digital technologies have brought about unprecedented changes in the media landscape. The proliferation of media platforms, the rise of social media, and the increasing accessibility of information have created opportunities and challenges for individuals and society.

The book examines how media shapes our understanding of popular culture, influencing fashion, music, and entertainment trends. It explores the impact of media on social relations, considering how digital platforms can both connect and isolate individuals. The intertwining of media and corporate capitalism is scrutinized, highlighting the commercial imperatives that often drive media production.

The book delves into the role of the media in democratic societies, considering its potential to serve as a watchdog, a platform for public debate, and a means of holding power to account. It critically examines the challenges of media bias, propaganda, and money's political influence.

The impact of new media on Indian society is explored, focusing on the rise of digital platforms and their influence on political communication, social engagement, and cultural expression. The challenges of misinformation, hate speech, and the digital divide are critically assessed.

The book concludes by considering the future of media in relation to consumerism, exploring how media shapes our consumption habits and identities. It emphasizes the importance of critical media literacy and advocates for educational approaches that empower individuals to navigate the complexities of media messages. The evolving landscape of media laws and regulations is examined, considering the balance between freedom of expression and the protection of public interest.

This book serves as a call to action, inviting readers to engage with media thoughtfully and critically, recognizing its power to shape our perceptions, values, and social realities. By understanding the complex interplay between media, culture, and society, we can become more informed consumers, responsible creators, and active participants in shaping a media landscape that reflects our shared humanity.

Willam Baskaran
Gandhigram 2024

Preface

In the tapestry of human existence, media has emerged as a powerful force, weaving its threads through the intricate layers of culture, society, and individual lives. From the ancient cave paintings that chronicled the lives of our ancestors to the pervasive digital screens that dominate our modern landscape, media has served as a mirror reflecting our values, beliefs, and aspirations.

This book, "Media/Social," explores the intricate relationship between these three pillars of human experience. It delves into the multifaceted ways in which media shapes and is shaped by the cultural and social contexts in which it operates. Through a sociological lens, we will examine the historical evolution of media, the theoretical frameworks that illuminate its influence, and the contemporary issues that challenge our understanding of its role in society.

A Historical Perspective: Tracing the Trajectory of Media

Our exploration begins by tracing the historical trajectory of media, from the invention of the printing press to the rise of digital platforms. Each technological advancement has brought about profound shifts in how we communicate, access information, and perceive the world. The printing press democratized knowledge, the radio, United Nations and television brought visual storytelling into our homes, and the internet created a global village, connecting individuals across vast distances.

As we examine this historical evolution, we will consider how each media era has shaped cultural production, social interactions, and power dynamics. By understanding the past, we gain insights into the present and can better anticipate the future of media and its impact on society.

Theoretical Foundations: Unveiling the Mechanisms of Influence

We will delve into the theoretical frameworks that have shaped media studies to fully grasp the complex interplay between media, culture, and society. These frameworks provide the tools to analyse how media operates within specific cultural and social contexts, revealing the mechanisms through which it exerts influence.

We will explore Marxist perspectives that critique media's role in perpetuating power dynamics and ideological control, highlighting how media ownership and content often serve the ruling class's interests. The Frankfurt School's critical theory will further illuminate how the culture industry can promote conformity and consumerism, shaping public consciousness to inhibit critical thought.

Our exploration will also encompass the work of Marshall McLuhan, whose assertion that "the medium is the message" challenges us to consider the profound effects of media technologies beyond their content. The rise of postmodernism will invite us to question contemporary media culture's fragmented and hyperreal nature, where the lines between reality and representation blur.

Contemporary Issues: Navigating the Complexities of the Digital Age

The rapid advancements in digital technologies have brought about unprecedented changes in the media landscape. The proliferation of media platforms, the rise of social media, and the increasing accessibility of information have created opportunities and challenges for individuals and society.

We will examine how media shapes our understanding of popular culture, influencing fashion, music, and entertainment trends. We will explore the impact of media on social relations, considering how digital platforms can both connect and isolate individuals. We will scrutinize the intertwining of media and corporate capitalism, highlighting the commercial imperatives that often drive media production.

Our exploration will also delve into the role of the media in democratic societies, considering its potential to serve as a watchdog, a platform for public debate, and a means of holding power to account. We will critically examine the challenges posed by media bias, propaganda, and the influence of money in politics.

The Indian Context: Media in a Diverse and Dynamic Society

With its rich cultural tapestry and complex social dynamics, India presents a unique context for understanding the interplay between media, culture, and society. We will examine how media operates within this diverse landscape, considering its role in shaping national identity, promoting regional cultures, and addressing social justice issues.

The Future of Media: Navigating a World of Constant Change

As we move further into the digital age, the media landscape continues to evolve at an unprecedented pace. Emerging technologies, shifting social dynamics, and global interconnectedness present challenges and opportunities for understanding and engaging with media.

We will consider the future of media in relation to consumerism, exploring how media shapes our consumption habits and identities. We will emphasize the importance of critical media literacy, advocating for educational approaches that empower individuals to navigate the complexities of media messages. We will examine the evolving landscape of media laws and regulations, considering the balance between freedom of expression and the protection of public interest.

A Call to Action: Engaging with Media Thoughtfully and Critically

This book is not merely an academic exercise but a call to action. It invites readers to engage with media thoughtfully and critically, recognizing its power to shape our perceptions, values, and social realities. By understanding the complex interplay between media, culture, and society, we can become more informed consumers, responsible creators, and active participants in shaping a media landscape that reflects our shared humanity.

ACKNOWLEDGEMENTS

I am incredibly thankful for the unwavering support, guidance, and inspiration from a remarkable group of individuals who have helped bring this book to life.

First and foremost, I extend my heartfelt gratitude to all the teachers whose invaluable mentorship and unwavering encouragement have guided me through the labyrinth of ideas, theories, and research that shaped this book. Your insightful feedback, constructive critiques, and unwavering belief in my potential have illuminated my path.

I would also like to express my sincere appreciation to the faculty and staff of the Department of Sociology at the Gandhigram Rural University, whose collective wisdom and unwavering dedication to fostering a vibrant intellectual community have nurtured my growth as a scholar.

Dear colleagues and friends in the Sociology program, I sincerely appreciate the time we've spent in enriching discussions and collaborative brainstorming. Your diverse perspectives and critiques have deepened my understanding of the connections between media, culture, and society. Thank you for your incredible support; it means a lot to me!

I am profoundly grateful to the countless scholars, researchers, and thinkers whose groundbreaking work has laid the foundation for media studies. Your profound insights, meticulous research, and unwavering dedication to unravelling the complexities of media's influence have inspired me to embark on this intellectual journey.

To my family and friends, whose unconditional love, solid support, and dogged belief in my dreams have been my constant source of strength, thank you from the bottom of my heart. Your unwavering encouragement has given me the courage to pursue my passions, and your stanch support has sustained me through the inevitable challenges along the way.

Finally, I would like to express my deepest gratitude to the countless individuals whose lived experiences, diverse perspectives, and unwavering engagement with media have shaped the very fabric of this book. Your stories, struggles, and triumphs have illuminated the profound impact of media on our lives, reminding me of the media's power to reflect and transform our shared existence.

In the spirit of acknowledging the collective effort that has culminated in this book, I extend my heartfelt thanks to the unsung heroes whose contributions may not be explicitly mentioned but whose dedication and hard work have been instrumental in making this project a reality.

To the editors, proofreaders, designers, and production team whose meticulous attention to detail and unwavering commitment to excellence have transformed my manuscript into a polished publication, I express my sincere appreciation. Your expertise and dedication have been invaluable in ensuring the quality and integrity of this work.

And to the readers who embark on this intellectual journey with me, I thank you for your curiosity, your willingness to engage with complex ideas and your unwavering belief in the power of media to shape our world. I sincerely hope this book will spark meaningful conversations, inspire critical thinking, and contribute to a deeper understanding of the intricate relationship between media, culture, and society.

R KUMARAN
Gandhigram, 2024

INTRODUCTION

In the intricate dance between human civilization and the tools we create, media has emerged as a compelling force, shaping and being shaped by the very fabric of our societies and cultures. This book, "Media, Culture, and Society," delves into the dynamic interplay between these three pillars of human experience, exploring how media intertwines with our lives to reflect, influence, and transform our shared existence.

From the ancient cave paintings that vividly captured the lives and imaginations of our ancestors to the ubiquitous digital screens that dominate our modern world, media has served as a mirror to society. It reflects our values, beliefs, and aspirations while simultaneously shaping our perceptions, identities, and social interactions. This book embarks on a journey to unravel this intricate relationship, examining the historical evolution of media, the theoretical frameworks that illuminate its influence, and the contemporary issues that challenge our understanding of its role in society.

A Historical Perspective: Tracing the Trajectory of Media

Our exploration begins by tracing the historical trajectory of media, from the invention of the printing press to the rise of digital platforms. Each technological advancement has brought about profound shifts in how we communicate, access information, and perceive the world around us. The printing press democratized knowledge, the radio united nations, television brought visual storytelling into our homes, and the internet created a global village, connecting individuals across vast distances.

As we examine this historical evolution, we will consider how each era of media has shaped cultural production, social interactions, and power dynamics. By understanding the past, we gain insights into the present and can better anticipate the future of media and its impact on society.

Theoretical Foundations: Unveiling the Mechanisms of Influence

To fully grasp the complex interplay between media, culture, and society, we will delve into the theoretical frameworks that have shaped media studies. These frameworks provide the tools to analyse how media operates within specific cultural and social contexts, revealing the mechanisms through which it exerts influence.

We will explore Marxist perspectives that critique media's role in perpetuating power dynamics and ideological control, highlighting how media ownership and content often serve the ruling class's interests. The Frankfurt School's critical theory will further illuminate how the culture industry can promote conformity and consumerism, shaping public consciousness to inhibit critical thought.

Our exploration will also encompass the work of Marshall McLuhan, whose assertion that "the medium is the message" challenges us to consider the profound effects of media technologies beyond their content. The rise of postmodernism will invite us to question contemporary media culture's fragmented and hyperreal nature, where the lines between reality and representation blur.

Contemporary Issues: Navigating the Complexities of the Digital Age

The rapid advancements in digital technologies have brought about unprecedented changes in the media landscape. The proliferation of media platforms, the rise of social media, and the increasing accessibility of information have created both opportunities and challenges for individuals and society.

We will examine how media shapes our understanding of popular culture, influencing fashion, music, and entertainment trends. The impact of media on social relations will be explored, considering how digital platforms can both connect and isolate individuals. The intertwining of media and corporate capitalism will be scrutinized, highlighting the commercial imperatives that often drive media production.

Our exploration will also delve into the role of media in democratic societies, considering its potential to serve as a watchdog, a platform for public debate, and a means of holding power to account. The challenges posed by media bias, propaganda, and the influence of money in politics will be critically examined.

The Indian Context: Media in a Diverse and Dynamic Society

India, with its rich cultural tapestry and complex social dynamics, presents a unique context for understanding the interplay between media, culture, and society. We will examine how media operates within this diverse landscape, considering its role in shaping national identity, promoting regional cultures, and addressing social justice issues.

The impact of new media on Indian society will be explored, focusing on the rise of digital platforms and their influence on political communication, social engagement, and cultural expression. The challenges posed by misinformation, hate speech, and the digital divide will be critically assessed.

The Future of Media: Navigating a World of Constant Change

As we move further into the digital age, the media landscape continues to evolve at an unprecedented pace. Emerging technologies, shifting social dynamics, and global interconnectedness present both challenges and opportunities for understanding and engaging with media.

We will consider the future of media in relation to consumerism, exploring how media shapes our consumption habits and identities. The importance of critical media literacy will be emphasized, advocating for educational approaches that empower individuals to navigate the complexities of media messages. The evolving landscape of media laws and regulations will be examined, considering the balance between freedom of expression and the protection of public interest.

The Structure of the Book

This book is structured to provide a comprehensive exploration of the interplay between media, culture, and society. It is organized into chapters, each focusing on a specific aspect of this relationship, guiding the reader through a multifaceted journey of understanding.

Chapter 1: Media and Society in Contemporary Society

This introductory chapter sets the stage for our exploration, providing an overview of the key themes and concepts that will be explored throughout the book. It emphasizes the importance of critically examining the role of media in our lives and outlines the structure and objectives of the book.

Defining Media, Culture, and Society

This chapter delves into the foundational definitions of media, culture, and society, clearly understanding these interconnected concepts. It explores the various forms of media, the characteristics of culture, and the dynamics of social structures, laying the groundwork for a deeper analysis of their interplay.

Historical Evolution of Media

This chapter traces the historical trajectory of media, examining the technological advancements and societal shifts that have shaped its evolution. From the invention of the printing press to the rise of digital platforms, we will explore how each era of media has influenced communication, culture, and power dynamics.

Chapter 2: Theoretical Foundations

This chapter delves into the theoretical frameworks that illuminate the complex relationship between media, culture, and society. We will explore Marxist perspectives, critical theory, McLuhan's ideas on media technology, postmodernism, and feminist critiques, providing a multifaceted lens through which to analyse media's influence.

Contemporary Issues in Media, Culture, and Society

This chapter examines contemporary issues that challenge our understanding of the media's role in society. We will explore the impact of media on popular culture, social relations, corporate capitalism, and democratic processes. We will also critically examine the challenges posed by media bias, propaganda, and the influence of money in politics.

Chapter 3: Media and Social Structure in India

This chapter focuses on India's unique context, exploring how media operates within its diverse and dynamic society. We will examine the media's role in shaping national identity, promoting regional cultures, and addressing social justice issues. We will also explore the impact of new media on Indian society, focusing on the rise of digital platforms and their influence on political communication, social engagement, and cultural expression.

Media and Audience in India

This chapter delves into the relationship between media and its audience in India, examining how audiences consume, interpret, and respond to media content. We will explore audience segmentation, media consumption patterns, and the implications for social engagement and cultural expression.

Media Ethics in India

This chapter examines the ethical considerations that arise in media production and consumption in India. We will explore the challenges faced by journalists and media organizations in upholding ethical standards, the role of self-regulation, and the impact of social media on ethical practices.

Chapter 4: Media Laws in India

This chapter provides an overview of the legal framework governing media operations in India. We will explore the historical development of media laws, current regulations, and the challenges that arise in a rapidly changing media environment.

Chapter 5: Media and Society: Praxis

This chapter focuses on the practical aspects of media production and consumption. We will explore media content creation, media appreciation, and critical media literacy, providing insights and tools for individuals to engage with media thoughtfully and responsibly.

CHAPTER I

MEDIA AND SOCIETY IN CONTEMPORARY SOCIETY

The relationship between media and society is multifaceted and dynamic, reflecting the complexities of contemporary social structures. Media, as both technology and social institutions, plays a pivotal role in shaping societal norms, values, and behaviours. From a sociological perspective, understanding this relationship requires a deep dive into the various elements that constitute media and communication, their historical evolution, and their impact on contemporary society. This essay will explore these aspects, drawing from Graeme Burton's "Media and Society: Critical Perspectives."

Media as Technology

Media technologies have significantly transformed over the past few decades, radically altering the communication landscape. From the advent of the printing press to the rise of digital media, each technological innovation has expanded the reach and influence of media.

Historical Evolution

The evolution of media technology can be traced back to Johannes Gutenberg's invention of the printing press in the mid-15th century. This innovation democratised access to information, enabling the mass production of books and the dissemination of knowledge. The 20th century saw the emergence of broadcast media, with radio and television becoming dominant forms of mass communication. These media brought about a shared cultural experience, creating a collective consciousness among audiences.

The rise of digital media and the internet has marked the late 20th and early 21st centuries. These technologies have increased the speed and volume of information exchange and facilitated interactive and participatory forms of communication. Social media platforms, in particular, have transformed how people communicate, allowing for real-time interaction and creating user-generated content.

Impact on Society

The impact of media technology on society is profound. It has reshaped how people access information, interact with one another, and perceive the world. Digital media's immediacy and ubiquity have blurred the lines between public and private spheres, creating new social dynamics and challenges.

Media technology also plays a crucial role in the economy, driving innovation and creating new business models. For example, the rise of digital advertising has transformed the marketing landscape, enabling more targeted and personalised advertising strategies.

Media as a Social Institution

Beyond technological aspects, media functions as a social institution, influencing and reflecting societal norms, values, and power structures. Media institutions, including newspapers, television networks, and online platforms, operate within a framework of economic, political, and cultural forces.

Economic Factors

Economic imperatives heavily influence media institutions. The drive for profit shapes the content and structure of media, often prioritising sensationalism and entertainment over substantive reporting. This media commercialisation has led to concerns about the quality and diversity of content available to audiences.

Moreover, media ownership is increasingly concentrated in the hands of a few conglomerates, raising issues of media pluralism and the representation of diverse viewpoints. This concentration of ownership can lead to a homogenisation of content and the marginalisation of minority voices.

Political Influence

The relationship between media and politics is complex and reciprocal. The media serves as a watchdog, holding political actors accountable and informing the public about political affairs. However, it can also be used as a tool for political propaganda and manipulation.

Governments and political actors often seek to influence media content and structure through regulation and ownership. In some cases, state control over media can lead to censorship and the suppression of dissenting voices. Conversely, a free and independent media is essential for a functioning democracy, providing a platform for diverse perspectives and fostering informed public debate.

Cultural Impact

Media plays a central role in the construction of cultural identities and social norms. Through representation and narrative, media shapes how individuals and groups perceive themselves and others. Issues of race, gender, and class are often mediated through media portrayals, influencing societal attitudes and behaviours.

The representation of marginalised groups in media has been a contentious issue, with concerns about stereotyping and misrepresentation. Positive and accurate representation can empower marginalised communities and promote social cohesion, while negative representation can reinforce prejudice and discrimination.

Elements of Media and Communication

To fully understand the relationship between media and society, it is essential to examine the key elements of media and communication: media institutions, texts, and audiences.

Media Institutions

Media institutions are the organisations responsible for the production, distribution, and regulation of media content. These institutions operate within a broader social, political, and economic context, influencing their structure and practices.

Key questions about media institutions include their role in society, their relationship with other dominant institutions (such as the advertising industry), and their understanding of their audiences. The power dynamics within media institutions and their influence on media content are also critical areas of inquiry.

Media Texts

Media texts refer to the content produced by media institutions, including news articles, television shows, films, advertisements, and social media posts. These texts are not merely reflections of reality but are constructed through selection and representation.

Analysing media texts involves examining their content, form, and meaning. This analysis can reveal underlying ideologies and power structures, as well as how media shapes and is shaped by societal norms and values.

Audiences

Audiences are the recipients of media texts, and their role in the media-society relationship is complex and multifaceted. Audiences are not passive consumers but actively interpret and engage with media content. Understanding audience behaviour involves examining how people access and use media, their interpretive strategies, and the social and cultural factors influencing media consumption. Audience research can provide insights into the impact of media on individual and collective identities, as well as how media can both reinforce and challenge social norms.

Media and Society in Contemporary Context

In contemporary society, the relationship between media and society is characterised by rapid technological change, increasing globalisation, and shifting power dynamics. The rise of digital and social media has transformed traditional media landscapes, creating new opportunities and challenges for media institutions, texts, and audiences.

Digital and Social Media

Digital and social media have revolutionised the way people communicate and access information. These platforms have democratised media production, allowing individuals to create and share content on a global scale. However, they have also raised concerns about misinformation, privacy, and the erosion of traditional media business models.

The interactive nature of digital media has given rise to new forms of participatory culture, where audiences are not just consumers but also producers of content. This shift has implications for media power dynamics, as traditional gatekeepers lose control over the flow of information.

Globalisation

Globalisation has expanded media reach, enabling the rapid dissemination of information across national boundaries. This global flow of media content has the potential to foster cross-cultural understanding and exchange. However, it also raises issues of cultural imperialism, where dominant cultures impose their values and norms on others.

The global media landscape is increasingly dominated by a few transnational corporations, leading to concerns about cultural homogenisation and the marginalisation of local media industries. The tension between global and local media is a crucial area of study in understanding the impact of globalisation on media and society.

Power and Regulation

Various forms of regulation shape the power dynamics within the media, including state policies, industry standards, and self-regulation by media organisations. Regulation is essential for ensuring media accountability and protecting the public interest. However, it can also be a tool for political control and censorship.

The balance between media freedom and regulation is a contentious issue, with debates about the extent to which media should be free from external influence. A diverse and independent media landscape is crucial for a healthy democracy and informed public discourse.

Understanding the Interplay between Media, Society and Culture

The intricate relationship between media, culture, and society is fundamental to contemporary life. In its various forms, media reflects and shapes the culture and social structures it operates. This book, "Media, Culture, and Society," explores these relationships by examining the historical evolution of media, its role in cultural production, and its impact on social institutions and individual identities. Through a multidisciplinary lens, we will delve into the theoretical foundations, contemporary issues, and future directions of media studies, providing a comprehensive understanding of how media influences and is influenced by culture and society.

Defining Media, Culture, and Society

Media

Media encompasses the various channels and platforms used to communicate information, ideas, and entertainment to a wide audience. It includes traditional forms such as print (newspapers, magazines), broadcast (radio, television), and digital (internet, social media). Media serves multiple functions: informing the public, providing entertainment, shaping public opinion, and facilitating social interaction.

Culture

Culture refers to the shared values, beliefs, practices, and artefacts characterising a group or society. It encompasses the arts, literature, music, traditions, and everyday practices that define a community's way of life. Culture is both a product of social interaction and a framework through which individuals understand their world and their place within it.

Society

Society is a structured community of individuals bound by social relationships and institutions. It encompasses the organised patterns of relationships and social arrangements that guide behaviour and interactions among its members. Societal structures include family, education, economy, politics, and religion, all of which are influenced by and interact with media and culture.

Historical Evolution of Media

The evolution of media can be traced through distinct historical phases, each marked by technological advancements and shifts in societal needs and expectations. Understanding this evolution provides context for analysing contemporary media landscapes.

Print Media

The invention of the printing press by Johannes Gutenberg in the mid-15th century marked the beginning of mass media. The ability to produce large quantities of books, pamphlets, and newspapers revolutionised the dissemination of information and ideas. Print media played a crucial role in the spread of the Renaissance, the Reformation, and the Enlightenment by making knowledge more accessible and challenging established authorities.

Broadcast Media

The 20th century saw the rise of broadcast media, beginning with radio and followed by television. Radio provided a new way to reach mass audiences with news, entertainment, and political messages, while television added a visual dimension that further enhanced its impact. The advent of broadcast media brought about significant changes in how information was consumed and influenced public opinion and cultural norms.

Digital Media

The late 20th and early 21st centuries witnessed the digital revolution, transforming the media landscape. The internet and digital technologies introduced new forms of media consumption, such as websites, social media platforms, and streaming services. Digital media has democratised content creation, allowing individuals and communities to produce and share their media, thereby challenging traditional gatekeepers of information.

Theoretical Foundations

Exploring the theoretical frameworks that have shaped media studies is essential to understanding the complex interplay between media, culture, and society. These theories provide tools for analysing how media operates within cultural and social contexts.

Functionalism

Functionalist theories view media as an integral part of society that performs essential functions, such as providing information, entertainment, and socialisation. Media helps maintain social order by reinforcing norms and values and by acting as a conduit for communication between different parts of society. Functionalism emphasises the positive contributions of media to societal stability and cohesion.

Marxian Theory

Marxian theories approach media from a critical perspective, focusing on its role in perpetuating power dynamics and ideological control. According to this view, media is an instrument of the ruling class, used to maintain their dominance by shaping public consciousness and reinforcing capitalist ideologies. Media content is seen as a commodity that reflects the interests of those who control its production and distribution.

Psychoanalytic Theory

Psychoanalytic theories explore the psychological effects of media on individuals and their unconscious motivations. This approach examines how media representations influence identity formation, desires, and fears. Psychoanalytic theory is particularly interested in media content's symbolic and emotional dimensions and psychological impact.

Critical Theory

Critical theory, particularly associated with the Frankfurt School, combines elements of Marxian and psychoanalytic theories to analyse media as a site of ideological struggle. Critical theorists argue that media perpetuates dominant ideologies and consumerist culture while marginalising alternative viewpoints. They advocate for a more emancipatory use of media that promotes critical thinking and social change.

Postmodernism

Postmodernist theories challenge traditional notions of media, culture, and society by emphasising contemporary media landscapes' fragmented and hyperreal nature. Postmodernism argues that media blurs the boundaries between reality and representation, creating a world where images and signs are more important than the underlying reality. This perspective highlights media's playful and fluid nature in shaping cultural and social meanings.

Feminist Theory

Feminist theories critique media for its representation of gender and its role in perpetuating patriarchal norms. Feminist media studies examine how media portrays women and men, the power dynamics involved in media production, and the impact of media on gender identities. Feminist theory advocates for more equitable and diverse representations in media, challenging stereotypes and promoting gender justice.

Contemporary Issues in Media, Culture, and Society

The rapid advancements in digital technologies and the proliferation of media platforms have brought about new challenges and opportunities in the media landscape. This section explores key contemporary issues shaping the relationship between media, culture, and society.

Media and Pop Culture

Popular culture, often called pop culture, is heavily mediated, with media playing a central role in its creation, dissemination, and consumption. Media shapes and reflects the public's tastes, values, and interests, influencing fashion, music, movies, and other cultural artefacts. The relationship between media and pop culture is dynamic, with media both driving and responding to cultural trends.

Media and Social Relations

Media significantly influences social interactions and relationships. Social media platforms, for example, have transformed how people communicate, build relationships, and form communities. While media can facilitate connections and foster social networks, it can also contribute to social isolation, cyberbullying, and the spread of misinformation.

Media and Corporate Capitalism

The media industry is deeply intertwined with corporate capitalism, with media corporations significantly shaping economic and political agendas. Media conglomerates control a vast array of media outlets, raising concerns about media concentration and the homogenisation of content. The commercial imperatives of media production often prioritise profit over public interest, influencing the nature and quality of media content.

Media and Democratic Polity

The media is a crucial component of democratic societies, serving as a watchdog, a platform for public debate, and a means of holding power to account. However, the relationship between media and democracy is complex, with issues such as media bias, propaganda, and money's political influence posing significant challenges. The role of the media in fostering an informed and engaged citizenry is critical for the health of democratic institutions.

Media and Liquid Modernity

As sociologist Zygmunt Bauman described, media reflects contemporary life's fluid and transient nature in the context of liquid modernity. Media content is characterised by its ephemerality and constant change, mirroring the instability and uncertainty of modern social and economic conditions. This perspective emphasises the need for adaptability and resilience in navigating the media-saturated world.

Media Popular Culture in Globalization and the Neo-Liberal Era

The processes of globalisation and neo-liberalism have had profound impacts on media and popular culture. Globalisation has facilitated the cross-cultural exchange of media content and created a global media culture while also raising concerns about cultural homogenisation and the dominance of Western media. Neo-liberal policies have led to the commercialisation and deregulation of media, prioritising market-driven approaches over public service and cultural diversity.

Future Directions in Media, Culture, and Society

As we move further into the digital age, the media, culture, and society landscape continues to evolve. Emerging technologies and changing social dynamics present challenges and opportunities for understanding and engaging with media.

Media and Consumerism

The relationship between media and consumerism remains a critical area of study. Media not only promotes consumer culture but also shapes consumer identities and lifestyles. Advertising, branding, and consumption practices are deeply embedded in media content, influencing individual and collective behaviours. In the Indian context, economic liberalisation and the rise of the middle class have transformed consumption patterns and media representations, making it an important area for further exploration.

Critical Media Literacy

Developing critical media literacy is essential for navigating the complex media landscape. Critical media literacy involves analysing and evaluating media content, understanding its underlying messages and intentions, and recognising the power dynamics involved in media production and consumption. Promoting critical media literacy is crucial for fostering informed and engaged citizens who can critically engage with media and advocate for more equitable and diverse media representations.

Media Laws and Regulation

Media regulation remains a contentious issue, balancing the need for freedom of expression with the protection of public interest. Media laws and policies vary across countries, reflecting different cultural, political, and social contexts. In India, media laws encompass a range of issues, including freedom of the press, censorship, and regulation of digital media. Understanding the legal frameworks governing media is essential for ensuring accountability and promoting ethical media practices.

New Media and Its Aftermath

The rise of new media has transformed the media landscape, raising questions about its impact on politics, culture, and society. Histories of new media highlight its rapid development and its challenges to traditional media. The politics of new media, including its role in political communication, election campaigns, and social movements, is a critical area of study. In the Indian context, the rise of new media has significantly influenced political communication and electoral behaviour, offering new avenues for engagement and activism.

The Influence of New Media on Indian Politics

Indian Media Economy

The Indian media economy has undergone substantial transformation with the advent of new media. Traditional media industries like print and broadcast have had to adapt to the changing landscape where digital platforms increasingly dominate. The rise of internet penetration and mobile phone usage in India has facilitated the growth of digital media, leading to a diversification of media consumption patterns. Online news portals, social media platforms, and streaming services have become integral parts of the Indian media ecosystem, offering content that caters to diverse linguistic, cultural, and demographic segments.

Changing Forms of Politics and Electoral Behaviour

New media has reshaped political communication in India, influencing electoral behaviour and campaign strategies. Social media platforms like Facebook, Twitter, and WhatsApp have become critical tools for political parties and candidates to reach and engage with voters. These platforms enable direct communication with constituents, bypassing traditional media gatekeepers and allowing real-time interaction and feedback. Data analytics and targeted advertising on social media have also become prevalent, enabling more personalised and effective campaign strategies. Social media is often used during elections to mobilise supporters, disseminate campaign messages, and counter opponents. For instance, the 2014 and 2019 general elections in India saw extensive social media use by political parties to influence public opinion and voter turnout. However, the rise of new media has also raised concerns about spreading misinformation, fake news, and manipulating public discourse through coordinated online campaigns.

Network and Cyber-Culture

The concept of network society, introduced by sociologist Manuel Castells, is pertinent in understanding the impact of new media on culture and society. Social, economic, and political processes are organised around digital networks in a network society, leading to new forms of social interaction and cultural production. Cyber-culture, encompassing the practices and norms associated with digital communities, reflects new media's dynamic and participatory nature.

Cyber-Culture and Digital Communities

Cyber-culture is characterised by the creation of digital communities that transcend geographical boundaries. Online forums, social media groups, and virtual worlds enable individuals to connect based on shared interests, identities, and goals. These digital communities foster new forms of social interaction, Collaboration, and cultural exchange. They also provide platforms for marginalised voices and alternative perspectives, challenging dominant cultural narratives and promoting diversity.

Video Games and Digital Entertainment

The rise of video games and digital entertainment has also been a significant aspect of new media culture. As interactive media, video games offer immersive experiences and have become a major cultural and economic force. The gaming industry in India has seen rapid growth, with increasing numbers of gamers and the proliferation of esports. Video games provide entertainment and influence cultural narratives and social interactions, creating new forms of storytelling and community building.

Digital Image and Social Media

The digital image, including photographs, videos, and memes, plays a central role in new media culture. Social media platforms facilitate creating, sharing, and consuming digital images, shaping how people present themselves and perceive others. Visual content is often used to convey identity, emotions, and opinions, making it a powerful tool for communication and cultural expression. The virality of digital images can amplify social movements, raise awareness of issues, and mobilise collective action.

Media and Consumerism

Mass Consumption and Commodity Culture

The relationship between media and consumerism is a critical study area, as media significantly promotes mass consumption and commodity culture. Advertising, branding, and marketing strategies are integral to media content, influencing consumer behaviour and shaping cultural values. Media promotes products and services and constructs lifestyles and identities around consumption.

Advertising, Consumption, and Branding

Advertising is a pervasive aspect of media, driving the economy of many media organisations. Through persuasive messages and visual appeals, advertising shapes consumer desires and creates demand for products and services. As a strategic approach to differentiate products, branding relies on media to build brand identity and loyalty. Media campaigns often employ narratives and imagery that resonate with cultural values and social aspirations, reinforcing consumer culture.

Consumption in the Indian Context

In India, economic liberalisation in the 1990s led to significant changes in consumption patterns and media representations. The rise of the Indian middle class and increased disposable income have fuelled consumerism, with media playing a key role in promoting new lifestyles and aspirations. Conspicuous consumption, characterised by the public display of wealth and status through material goods, has become a prominent feature of Indian society. Media representations of luxury brands, celebrity endorsements, and aspirational lifestyles contribute to the culture of consumption.

Consumer Citizenship

Consumer citizenship is the idea that individuals express their identities and exercise their rights and responsibilities through consumption choices. Media influences consumer citizenship by shaping perceptions of ethical consumption, sustainability, and social responsibility. Campaigns promoting fair trade, eco-friendly products, and corporate social responsibility highlight the role of media in encouraging consumers to consider the broader social and environmental impact of their purchases.

Ecological Citizenship and Ecohabitus

Ecological citizenship extends the concept of consumer citizenship to encompass environmental considerations. Media is crucial in raising awareness of ecological issues and promoting sustainable practices. Ecohabitus, a term derived from Pierre Bourdieu's concept of habitus, refers to the dispositions and practices related to environmental sustainability that are shaped by media representations and cultural norms. Developing critical media literacy around ecological citizenship involves understanding how media constructs environmental narratives and encourages sustainable consumption.

Media Appreciation and Critical Media Literacy

Developing Critical Media Literacy

Critical media literacy involves the ability to analyse, evaluate, and create media content with an understanding of its underlying messages, intentions, and power dynamics. It encompasses critical thinking, media analysis, and ethical reasoning skills. Developing critical media literacy is essential for navigating the complex media landscape, recognising biases, and engaging with media as informed and active citizens.

Media Appreciation

Media appreciation involves understanding and valuing media content's aesthetic, cultural, and social dimensions. It includes recognising the artistic and technical aspects of media production and the cultural significance and impact of media representations. Media appreciation fosters a deeper engagement with media, encouraging critical reflection and meaningful interaction with diverse forms of media content.

Media Laws and Regulations in India

Media and the IPC and the CRPC

In India, media is governed by various legal frameworks, including the Indian Penal Code (IPC) and the Code of Criminal Procedure (CRPC). These laws address issues such as defamation, obscenity, and incitement to violence, ensuring that media content adheres to ethical and legal standards. The regulation of media is aimed at balancing freedom of expression with the protection of public interest and maintaining social harmony.

Self-Regulation

Self-regulation refers to the media industry's efforts to govern itself through codes of conduct, ethical guidelines, and industry standards. Media organisations and associations often establish self-regulatory bodies to monitor and address issues related to content quality, accuracy, and ethical practices. In India, the Press Council of India and the News Broadcasting Standards Authority are examples of self-regulatory bodies that oversee print and broadcast media, respectively.

Print Media and the Origins of Press Laws

The regulation of print media in India originates in colonial-era press laws, which were initially implemented to control dissent and maintain colonial authority. Post-independence, these laws were reformed to protect freedom of the press and ensure responsible journalism. The Press and Registration of Books Act of 1867 and the Press Council Act of 1978 are key legislations that govern the functioning of print media in India.

Broadcast Media: Evolution and Challenges to Policy

Broadcast media in India has evolved significantly since the inception of radio and television. The government initially controlled broadcast media, with All India Radio (AIR) and Doordarshan being the primary state-run broadcasters. The liberalisation of the media sector in the 1990s led to the proliferation of private television channels and radio stations, raising new challenges for media regulation. Issues such as content regulation, licensing, and media ownership remain critical areas of policy debate.

Internet and the New Media Policy

The rise of the internet and digital media has necessitated new regulatory frameworks to address the unique challenges posed by online content. The Information Technology (IT) Act of 2000 and subsequent amendments provide the legal basis for regulating Internet activities in India. The new media policy aims to address issues such as online privacy, cybercrime, and the regulation of digital platforms, balancing innovation and freedom of expression with the need for accountability and security.

Media Law and Women

Media law in India also addresses issues related to the representation and treatment of women in media. Laws and guidelines aim to prevent the portrayal of women in derogatory or stereotypical ways, promote gender-sensitive content, and protect women from harassment and exploitation in the media industry. The National Commission for Women (NCW) and various women's rights organisations advocate for more equitable and respectful representations of women in media.

Conclusion

The interplay between media, culture, and society is a complex and dynamic process that shapes and is shaped by technological advancements, cultural norms, and social structures. This book, "Media, Culture, and Society," aims to comprehensively understand this interplay by exploring the historical evolution of media, theoretical foundations, contemporary issues, and future directions. By examining the multifaceted relationships between media, culture, and society, we can better appreciate the role of media in our lives and its potential to influence social change, cultural production, and individual identities.

Understanding Mass Media

Mass media refers to various platforms and technologies used to communicate with a large audience. These platforms include print media (newspapers, magazines), broadcast media (radio, television), digital media (internet, social media), and traditional media (folk and community media). Mass media serves as a vehicle for information dissemination, education, entertainment, and persuasion. Its primary goal is to reach a broad audience, often simultaneously, using different formats and channels.

Evolution of Mass Media

1. **Print Media**

   Early Beginnings: The advent of the printing press by Johannes Gutenberg in the mid-15th century marked the beginning of mass media. The printing press revolutionized the production of books, making them more accessible and affordable.

   Newspapers and Magazines: In the 17th and 18th centuries, newspapers and magazines emerged as prominent forms of print media, providing news, opinions, and serialized literature to the public.

2. **Broadcast Media**

   Radio: The early 20th century saw the rise of radio as a significant mass medium. Radio broadcasts could reach a wide audience instantly, making it a powerful tool for news dissemination and entertainment.

   Television: Television followed radio, combining visual and auditory elements. By the mid-20th century, television became the dominant form of mass media, offering a variety of programs, including news, dramas, and comedies.

3. **Digital Media**

   Internet: The late 20th century introduced the internet, transforming the media landscape. The internet enabled instant global communication and access to vast information.

   Social Media: Platforms like Facebook, Twitter, and Instagram have further revolutionized mass media, allowing for user-generated content and interactive communication.

4. **Traditional Media**

   Folk and Community Media: Despite the dominance of modern technologies, traditional media like folk songs, storytelling, and community gatherings continue to play a vital role, especially in rural and indigenous communities.

Key Characteristics of Mass Media

1. **Reach and Accessibility**

   Mass media has the capability to reach a vast audience, transcending geographical boundaries. Whether through print, broadcast, or digital platforms, mass media can disseminate information to millions of people simultaneously. For example, television broadcasts can be viewed by people across different continents, while social media posts can go viral globally within minutes.

2. **Immediacy and Timeliness**

   One of the defining characteristics of mass media is its ability to provide immediate and timely information. News updates, weather forecasts, and live event coverage keep the public informed in real-time. For instance, during natural disasters, mass media plays a crucial role in delivering urgent information and safety instructions to the public.

3. **Public Nature**

   Mass media operates in the public domain, making information accessible to anyone with access to the medium. This public nature ensures that a wide audience can receive the same information, contributing to shared knowledge and experiences. For example, a major sporting event broadcasted on television can be watched by millions of fans around the world simultaneously.

4. **Content Diversity**

   Mass media offers a diverse range of content to cater to various interests and preferences. This includes news, entertainment, educational programs, advertisements, and more. For instance, television channels offer a wide array of programs, from documentaries and news reports to reality shows and sitcoms.

5. Technological Dependency

The functioning of mass media relies heavily on technological advancements. From the printing press to the internet, technological innovations have continually shaped and transformed mass media. For example, the development of digital streaming services like Netflix and YouTube has revolutionized how people consume media content, allowing for on-demand viewing and personalized recommendations.

6. Economic Influence

Mass media is significantly influenced by economic factors, including advertising revenue and corporate ownership. Media organizations often depend on advertising as a primary source of income, shaping the content they produce and broadcast. For instance, television networks generate substantial revenue through commercial advertisements, which in turn influences programming decisions and scheduling.

7. Regulation and Control

Mass media is subject to varying degrees of regulation and control by governments and regulatory bodies to ensure ethical standards, accuracy, and public interest. This includes laws related to censorship, broadcasting rights, and content restrictions. For example, the Federal Communications Commission (FCC) in the United States regulates broadcast media to ensure that content adheres to certain standards of decency and accuracy.

8. Interactive Potential

With the advent of digital media, interactivity has become a key characteristic of mass media. Social media platforms, online forums, and interactive websites enable users to engage with content, share opinions, and participate in discussions. For instance, social media platforms allow users to comment on news articles, share personal stories, and engage in real-time conversations with content creators and other users.

9. Globalization and Localization

Mass media operates on both global and local levels, addressing the needs and interests of diverse audiences. Globalization has allowed media content to cross borders, creating a global culture. Simultaneously, localization ensures that media content is relevant and relatable to local audiences. For example, international news networks like CNN and BBC provide global news coverage, while local newspapers and radio stations focus on community-specific issues and events.

10. Agenda-Setting Function

Mass media has the power to shape public discourse by highlighting certain issues and topics, thus influencing the public agenda. This agenda-setting function determines what issues are considered important and worthy of public attention. For example, extensive media coverage of climate change has brought the issue to the forefront of public and political discourse, prompting discussions and actions at various levels.

Understanding the characteristics of mass media is essential for comprehending its role and influence in contemporary society. From its evolution through various technological advancements to its ability to reach and engage diverse audiences, mass media continues to be a powerful tool for communication, education, and entertainment. By recognizing these characteristics, we can better appreciate the complexities and dynamics of mass media and its impact on our daily lives.

The History and Evolution of Print Media

The Invention of the Printing Press

The history of print media is often traced back to the invention of the printing press by Johannes Gutenberg in the mid-15th century. Before this revolutionary invention, books were painstakingly copied by hand, a process that was labour-intensive and time-consuming, making books expensive and scarce. Gutenberg's printing press, with its movable type, allowed for the mass production of texts, drastically reducing the cost and increasing the availability of printed materials. This innovation is widely regarded as a catalyst for the Renaissance, the Reformation, and the Scientific Revolution, as it enabled the widespread dissemination of knowledge and ideas.

Early Printed Books

Gutenberg's first major print project was the Gutenberg Bible, completed around 1455. This landmark publication demonstrated the potential of the printing press to produce high-quality, uniform copies of texts. The success of the Gutenberg Bible paved the way for the proliferation of printed books, which began to appear in various European cities. By the end of the 15th century, printing presses were established in over 200 cities across Europe, producing millions of books and transforming the landscape of knowledge and communication.

The Rise of Newspapers

Early Newspapers

The evolution of print media continued with the emergence of newspapers in the early 17th century. The first newspapers were small, one-page sheets that reported on local events and were often distributed weekly. One of the earliest known newspapers is the "Relation," published in Strasbourg in 1605 by Johann Carolus. These early newspapers were typically funded by wealthy patrons and were limited in circulation, but they set the stage for the development of more widespread news dissemination.

Expansion and Commercialization

The 18th century saw the expansion and commercialization of newspapers. With the rise of the middle class and increasing literacy rates, there was a growing demand for news and information. In England, the "Daily Courant," published in 1702, became the first daily newspaper, setting a precedent for regular news updates. In America, Benjamin Franklin's "Pennsylvania Gazette," founded in 1728, played a significant role in the development of American journalism by combining news with opinion pieces and advertisements.

The Golden Age of Print Media

19th Century Advancements

The 19th century is often referred to as the golden age of print media. Several key developments during this period contributed to the growth and influence of print media:

- **Technological Innovations:** The invention of the steam-powered printing press by Friedrich Koenig in 1810 and the rotary press by Richard March Hoe in 1843 dramatically increased the speed and efficiency of printing. These innovations allowed for the mass production of newspapers and books, making them more affordable and accessible to the general public.

- **Penny Press:** The introduction of the penny press in the 1830s revolutionized the newspaper industry. Newspapers like "The Sun," founded by Benjamin Day in 1833, sold for just one cent, making them accessible to a wider audience. The penny press focused on human interest stories, crime, and sensational news, appealing to the masses and increasing newspaper circulation.

- **Illustrations and Photography:** The development of lithography and later advancements in photography allowed for the inclusion of images in newspapers and magazines. Illustrated newspapers like "Harper's Weekly," founded in 1857, combined detailed illustrations with news stories, enhancing the visual appeal and impact of print media.

Magazines and Periodicals

In addition to newspapers, the 19th century also saw the rise of magazines and periodicals. Magazines like "The Gentleman's Magazine" (1731) and "The Tatler" (1709) catered to the interests of specific audiences, offering a mix of essays, fiction, and commentary. By the late 19th century, magazines such as "National Geographic" (1888) and "Vogue" (1892) had established themselves as influential publications, covering topics ranging from science and exploration to fashion and lifestyle.

The 20th Century and Beyond

Mass Media and the Role of Print

The 20th century brought about significant changes in the landscape of print media, influenced by technological advancements and the rise of new forms of mass media:

- **Radio and Television:** The advent of radio in the 1920s and television in the 1950s introduced new competition for print media. While newspapers and magazines continued to play a crucial role in providing in-depth news and analysis, radio and television offered instant news updates and live coverage, changing the way people consumed information.

- **Tabloid Journalism:** The early 20th century saw the rise of tabloid journalism, characterized by sensationalism and an emphasis on entertainment. Newspapers like "The Daily Mirror" in the UK and "The New York Daily News" in the US adopted a tabloid format, featuring bold headlines, large photographs, and human interest stories. This approach attracted a broad readership and influenced the style of modern journalism.

- **Digital Revolution:** The late 20th and early 21st centuries witnessed the digital revolution, transforming the print media industry. The rise of the internet and digital publishing platforms posed challenges to traditional print media, as online news sources offered real-time updates and interactive content. Many newspapers and magazines transitioned to digital formats, establishing online editions and embracing multimedia storytelling.

The Future of Print Media

Despite the challenges posed by digital media, print media continues to evolve and adapt. Niche magazines, literary journals, and independent newspapers have found ways to thrive by catering to specific interests and maintaining high-quality content. Print media's tactile experience, credibility, and ability to provide in-depth analysis and long-form journalism remain valued by readers.

The Emergence of Electronic Media: Radio and Television

The early 20th century marked the inception of electronic media, with radio emerging as a potent new medium of communication. The ability to transmit sound wirelessly across vast distances revolutionized information dissemination, bringing news, entertainment, and cultural experiences into homes and communities worldwide. Radio cultivated a collective experience, uniting nations and establishing a global community where individuals could engage through the airwaves.

Television emerged, introducing a visual aspect to electronic media and further altering the media landscape. The capacity to convey images and sound into residences fostered an immersive experience, integrating the world into the living room and influencing individual perceptions of reality. Television emerged as a formidable influence in the formation of popular culture, impacting fashion, music, and entertainment trends. It significantly influenced political communication, allowing leaders to directly engage with the public and mould public opinion on pivotal issues.

The Digital Revolution: The Internet and Its Implications

The late 20th century marked the onset of the digital revolution, with the internet becoming a pivotal influence in media and communication. The internet's capacity to link individuals and communities over extensive distances established a global network for the instantaneous exchange of information. The proliferation of personal computers and mobile devices has democratised information access, enabling individuals to create, consume, and disseminate content in unparalleled manners.

The internet has facilitated the emergence of social media platforms, which serve as potent instruments for communication, social interaction, and community development. Social media has facilitated connections among individuals with similar interests, allowed for the sharing of experiences, and promoted public discourse on a global level. Nonetheless, it has also elicited apprehensions regarding misinformation, echo chambers, and the degradation of privacy.

The Indian Context: Electronic and Digital Media in a Diverse Society

In India, the impact of electronic and digital media has been particularly profound, given the country's vast population, cultural diversity, and complex social dynamics. Radio and television have played a crucial role in uniting the nation, promoting regional cultures, and disseminating information to even the most remote corners of the country. The rise of digital media has further democratized access to information, empowering marginalized communities and providing a platform for diverse voices. However, the rise of new media has also presented unique challenges, including the spread of misinformation, the formation of echo chambers, and concerns about online privacy and surveillance.

Theoretical Frameworks: Understanding the Impact of Electronic and Digital Media

Several theoretical frameworks have emerged to help us understand the profound impact of electronic and digital media on society and culture.

Technological Determinism: This perspective emphasizes the role of technology in shaping social change, arguing that new media technologies have inherent characteristics that influence how we think, communicate, and interact. McLuhan's concept of "the medium is the message" exemplifies this approach, suggesting that the form of media itself, rather than its content, is the primary driver of its impact.

Social Construction of Technology: This perspective challenges technological determinism, arguing that social factors, rather than technological ones, are the primary drivers of media's impact. It emphasizes how individuals and communities actively shape the use and meaning of media technologies, highlighting the role of culture, power dynamics, and social norms in shaping media's influence.

Network Society: This concept, developed by Manuel Castells, emphasizes the transformative impact of digital networks on social structures and power dynamics. It argues that digital networks have created a new form of social organization, where information and communication flows are decentralised and power is distributed more horizontally.

Media Ecology: This approach examines media as environments, recognizing that different media create different social and cultural contexts. It underscores the interdependence of media, technology, and culture, contending that alterations in one domain invariably precipitate modifications in others.

The Prospects of Electronic and Digital Media

As we progress deeper into the digital era, the future of electronic and digital media is characterised by both potential and ambiguity. Emerging technologies, including artificial intelligence, virtual reality, and the Internet of Things, are set to further revolutionise the media landscape, generating new opportunities for communication, creativity, and social interaction. Nonetheless, these advancements also elicit apprehensions regarding ethical implications, privacy, and the possibility of abuse.

In traversing this dynamic environment, it is essential to embrace a critical viewpoint, acknowledging the influence of electronic and digital media on our perceptions, values, and social realities. By comprehending the historical trajectory, theoretical frameworks, and current challenges, we can interact with media judiciously and responsibly, leveraging its capacity for positive social transformation while alleviating its potential hazards.

Final Assessment

The emergence of electronic and digital media has initiated a transformative period in human communication, altering the dynamics of culture, society, and personal experience. The unifying influence of radio and the democratising impact of the internet have fundamentally transformed our methods of connection, creation, and information consumption through electronic and digital media.

As we traverse the intricacies of this constantly changing environment, it is essential to embrace a critical viewpoint, acknowledging the significant impact of electronic and digital media on our existence. By comprehending its historical development, theoretical constructs, and current challenges, we can interact with media judiciously and responsibly, leveraging its capacity for beneficial social transformation while alleviating its inherent risks.

Marshall McLuhan stated, "We shape our tools, and subsequently, our tools shape us." As we develop electronic and digital media tools, let us proceed with awareness, critical engagement, and a dedication to cultivating a media ecosystem that empowers individuals, fortifies communities, and advances a more just and equitable society.

Comprehensive Analysis of the Indian Media Landscape

To gain a comprehensive understanding of the intricacies of electronic and digital media's impact in India, let us examine particular facets in greater detail:

The Enduring Legacy of Radio: Despite the emergence of newer media, radio maintains a significant role in Indian society, particularly in rural regions with restricted internet access. Its capacity to overcome literacy obstacles and engage various linguistic communities renders it an effective instrument for information dissemination, education, and entertainment. Initiatives centred on agriculture, health, and social concerns enhance rural development and empower communities. Television's Pervasive Influence: Television has infiltrated the Indian cultural landscape, influencing entertainment, news consumption, and social norms. Television, encompassing mythological epics such as the Ramayana and Mahabharata as well as reality shows and soap operas, both mirrors and shapes societal values, aspirations, and consumer behaviour. Its significance in political communication is paramount, as televised debates, election campaigns, and news coverage influence public opinion and political discourse. •

Digital India: Prospects and Obstacles: India's swift embrace of digital technologies has created unparalleled prospects for economic expansion, social inclusion, and information accessibility. Government initiatives such as Digital India seek to close the digital divide and utilise technology for advancement. The proliferation of mobile internet access has been notably transformative, linking millions to online services, e-commerce, and social media. Nonetheless, obstacles persist in guaranteeing equitable access, digital literacy, and online safety.

The Influence of Social Media on Indian Society: Social media platforms have become essential to Indian life, enabling social interaction, political mobilisation, and cultural expression. They offer a platform for varied perspectives, facilitate community development, and empower under-represented groups. Nonetheless, the proliferation of misinformation, hate speech, and online harassment presents considerable challenges. The influence of social media on political discourse and electoral outcomes is an increasingly significant concern.

The Indian media landscape is perpetually evolving, characterised by the emergence of new platforms and technologies. Streaming services are revolutionising entertainment consumption, online news platforms are contesting conventional media, and mobile-centric content creation is proliferating. This evolving landscape necessitates ongoing adjustment and rigorous assessment to manage the intricacies of media's impact in India.

Confronting the Challenges and Leveraging the Potential

The revolution in electronic and digital media offers both prospects and obstacles for India. To leverage its capacity for beneficial social transformation, it is essential to tackle fundamental issues:

Bridging the Digital Divide: Ensuring equitable access to technology and digital literacy for all citizens is essential to avert further marginalisation and enable individuals to engage fully in the digital economy.

Promoting Media Literacy: Cultivating critical thinking abilities and media literacy is vital for countering misinformation, encouraging responsible media consumption, and enabling citizens to adeptly navigate the intricacies of the digital landscape.

Ensuring Online Safety: It is imperative to tackle online harassment, cyberbullying, and data privacy concerns to establish a secure and inclusive digital environment for everyone.

Promoting Ethical Media Practices: Advocating for ethical journalism, responsible content creation, and media accountability is crucial for sustaining public trust and ensuring that media serves the public interest. By proactively confronting these challenges and cultivating a critical and responsible media approach, India can leverage the transformative potential of electronic and digital media to advance social progress, economic development, and cultural enrichment for all its citizens.

This comprehensive examination of the history of electronic and digital media, particularly within the Indian context, offers an enhanced comprehension of its intricate relationship with culture and society. By analysing the historical trajectory, theoretical frameworks, and current challenges, we can critically and consciously engage with this potent force, thereby shaping a media landscape that empowers individuals, fortifies communities, and fosters a more just and equitable society.

The Influence of Mass Media on Individuals, Society, and Culture

Mass media exerts considerable influence in moulding the perceptions, beliefs, and behaviours of individuals, communities, and entire societies. Media, whether via newspapers, radio, television, or digital platforms, plays a crucial role in disseminating information, shaping cultural norms, and either reinforcing or contesting social structures. As media progresses, its societal role amplifies, impacting individual identity development and collective perspectives on politics, economics, and social matters. The sociological ramifications of media influence permeate individual psychology, social dynamics, and cultural values, rendering it an essential domain of inquiry for comprehending contemporary society.

The Impact of Media on Individuals: Identity, Perception, and Behaviour

The media profoundly influences individual identity and self-concept. Individuals develop their self-perception and worldview by assimilating messages communicated through media. Media not only informs but also shapes individuals' attitudes, beliefs, and aspirations, influencing their self-perception and perceptions of others.

An exemplary illustration of this is the "social comparison theory," posited by social psychologist Leon Festinger, which asserts that individuals assess themselves relative to others. When media showcases idealised representations of beauty, success, or lifestyle, it prompts individuals to evaluate their self-worth against these benchmarks, frequently resulting in unrealistic expectations and discontent. This is apparent in India's flourishing film and advertising sectors, where depictions of beauty and success are aspirational but frequently unattainable for the majority of the populace. The influence of these representations is particularly significant among adolescents, who are susceptible to media-induced expectations, potentially resulting in body image dissatisfaction and self-esteem difficulties.

The psychological impacts of media have intensified in the digital era, especially due to the pervasive influence of social media. Platforms such as Instagram, Twitter, and Facebook facilitate continuous connectivity and visibility into others' lives, engendering a sensation of perpetual scrutiny. Sociologists observe that this cultivates a culture of performativity, wherein individuals meticulously curate their identities and experiences to conform to societal expectations and obtain validation through likes, comments, and shares. This results in the phenomenon of "impression management," as articulated by Erving Goffman, wherein individuals continuously modify their behaviours and presentations in response to social feedback, obscuring the distinction between genuine self-expression and public persona.

The Role of Mass Media in Shaping and Reinforcing Cultural Norms

In addition to personal impact, media significantly shapes cultural norms and values, influencing societal definitions of acceptable behaviour, beauty standards, gender roles, and moral principles. Media scholar Stuart Hall's theory of "encoding and decoding" elucidates that media content is not impartial; it is "encoded" with particular meanings by producers, which audiences subsequently "decode" according to their cultural contexts and experiences. This encoding-decoding process establishes a cultural feedback loop, wherein media both mirrors and reinforces societal values.

In India, television serials and Bollywood films illustrate how media sustains cultural narratives regarding family dynamics, gender roles, and social hierarchies. Traditional soap operas frequently underscore the significance of familial loyalty, matrimony, and reverence for elders, thereby reinforcing cultural norms that prioritise collectivism and obligation. Historically, Bollywood films have depicted idealised gender roles, portraying men as robust protectors and women as devoted caretakers. These representations influence societal norms regarding masculinity and femininity, affecting how individuals perform gender roles in their personal lives.

Nonetheless, media can function as a medium for contesting cultural norms and presenting alternative viewpoints. Recent transformations in Indian cinema and television encompass representations of non-conventional family dynamics, LGBTQ+ relationships, and matters such as caste discrimination. By mainstreaming these topics, media can shape cultural attitudes, potentially promoting greater acceptance and progressive social change. The "agenda-setting" function of media, a concept formulated by Maxwell McCombs and Donald Shaw, demonstrates how media emphasis on particular issues shapes public discourse and alters societal priorities. By amplifying marginalised voices and issues, media possesses the capacity to challenge conventional hierarchies and foster cultural transformation.

Media as a Catalyst for Socialisation

Sociologists assert that media serves as a potent agent of socialisation, influencing individuals' values, norms, and behaviours from an early age. In conjunction with family, peers, and educational institutions, media imparts knowledge regarding societal expectations, role models, and life aspirations. The media constructs narratives regarding success, desirability, and morality through stories, advertisements, and news coverage. In India, where media accessibility is rapidly increasing, even rural populations are progressively impacted by mass media, undergoing socialisation that connects urban and rural divides and introduces them to varied lifestyles and perspectives.

A notable sociological perspective on this phenomenon is cultivation theory, introduced by George Gerbner, which asserts that extended exposure to media, especially television, fosters a skewed perception of reality. Gerbner's research indicated that frequent television viewers frequently acquire a "mean world syndrome," leading them to perceive the world as more perilous and violent than it truly is, attributable to the sensational portrayal of crime and violence in media. This theory is applicable in India to both television and digital news consumption, where reporting on communal violence, crime, and political conflicts may engender an increased sense of insecurity among viewers. This perceived reality affects both individual and societal attitudes regarding crime, security, and trust in social institutions.

The Media's Function in Social Cohesion and Fragmentation

The media possesses the distinct ability to either unify or fragment societies, contingent upon the narratives it disseminates and the manner in which audiences interact with it. Media can act as a unifying force, fostering a shared experience that enhances national identity and cultural cohesion. Major events like national holidays, sporting events, or important political speeches disseminated through media platforms cultivate communal emotions and a feeling of collective identity. In India, cricket matches and national observances such as Republic Day and Independence Day serve as occasions for collective participation, bolstering national pride and a shared identity.

Conversely, media possesses the capacity to exacerbate social divisions. Sociologists have noted that sensationalised coverage of sensitive subjects, including religion, caste, and regional identities, can intensify pre-existing social tensions. The "media framing" theory, introduced by sociologist Robert Entman, elucidates how media frames—by emphasising particular facets of a narrative—affect public perception. By categorising specific groups as "outsiders" or "threats," the media can cultivate prejudice and social exclusion, exacerbating societal divisions. In India, media representations that accentuate division over unity occasionally exacerbate communal tensions and caste conflicts, influencing public perception and intergroup dynamics.

Political Economy of Media: Proprietorship, Advertising, and Content

The political economy of media—encompassing the interplay between media ownership, economic interests, and content—also determines media's impact on society. In capitalist societies, media organisations function within a commercial paradigm, where profit incentives propel content production and distribution. This relationship is essential in ascertaining which issues are covered, whose perspectives are elevated, and how information is presented. Herbert Schiller noted that media dominated by corporate entities frequently favours narratives that coincide with corporate and political interests, often undermining critical journalism and social responsibility.

In India, this is especially pertinent as prominent media conglomerates, controlled by influential business entities, dominate editorial choices. Dependence on advertising revenue influences media content, as outlets may engage in self-censorship to prevent offending advertisers or powerful stakeholders. For example, coverage of labour rights, environmental degradation, or corporate malfeasance may be minimised if these subjects contradict advertisers' interests. This dynamic prompts ethical enquiries regarding the media's function in society and the degree to which it can authentically fulfil the public interest.

Globalisation and Cultural Imperialism

Globalisation has broadened the scope of media, enabling cross-cultural exchange while simultaneously provoking apprehensions regarding cultural imperialism. Western media, especially that of the United States, exerts considerable global influence, shaping cultural values, lifestyles, and consumer behaviour internationally. Herbert Schiller, a sociologist, contended that cultural imperialism transpires when dominant nations disseminate their media and cultural products, subsequently monopolising local markets and undermining indigenous cultures.

The influx of Western media in India, including Hollywood films, Western music, and international television shows, has introduced novel ideas and lifestyles, particularly among urban youth. This exposure fosters cultural diversity but also threatens traditional values and practices, resulting in tension between global and local identities. Younger generations may embrace Western perspectives on relationships, fashion, and individualism, thereby contesting traditional family structures and societal norms in Indian culture. The concept of "glocalization," introduced by sociologist Roland Robertson, denotes the amalgamation of global and local cultures, wherein individuals incorporate global influences into local settings.

Digital Media, Technological Innovations, and Emerging Forms of Social Authority

The emergence of digital media and technological innovations has altered the power dynamics within the media landscape, decentralising content creation and distribution. In contrast to traditional media, where content is generated by a restricted number of organisations, digital platforms enable individuals to independently create and disseminate content. This transformation has democratised media, enabling citizens to engage as active participants instead of passive consumers. In India, this is evident in the proliferation of social media influencers, citizen journalism, and grassroots movements that utilise digital platforms to engage extensive audiences.

Digital media has facilitated novel manifestations of social power. Through "hashtag activism" and viral campaigns, individuals and movements can shape public discourse, exert pressure on policymakers, and highlight issues overlooked by mainstream media. Global movements such as #MeToo and #BlackLivesMatter have significantly impacted public opinion and policy. In India, initiatives such as #JusticeForDalits and the farmer protests demonstrate how digital platforms enable collective action, empowering marginalised groups to organise and express their grievances.

Nonetheless, the digital environment presents challenges such as the proliferation of misinformation, the existence of echo chambers, and heightened surveillance. Social media algorithms favour sensational content, thereby amplifying divisive messages, reinforcing biases, and diminishing opportunities for constructive dialogue. Furthermore, the dependence of digital media on user data engenders apprehensions regarding privacy and surveillance, as individuals' online activities are monitored, evaluated, and commercialised. The surveillance-capitalist model, as critiqued by Shoshana Zuboff, illustrates how digital media alters power dynamics by commodifying personal data, impacting individual autonomy and societal governance.

Navigating the Influence of Media in Contemporary Society

The influence of mass media on individuals, society, and culture is intricate, diverse, and continually evolving with technological progress. Media informs, entertains, socialises, divides, and unites, acting as both a reflection and a shaper of societal values. Comprehending the sociological influence of media necessitates a critical awareness of the factors that shape media content, the effects on individual psychology and cultural norms, and the wider implications for democratic participation.

As media evolves, cultivating media literacy is crucial for individuals and societies to navigate its influence responsibly. By adopting a critical stance towards media consumption, individuals can alleviate the adverse effects of media, fostering a society in which media upholds the public interest, honours diversity, and enhances informed democratic engagement.

Media, Society, and Technology – Transformations and Impacts

The interaction among media, society, and technology is a crucial factor influencing contemporary social existence. The progression of media technologies—from the printing press to television, the internet, and currently AI-driven platforms—has transformed the ways in which individuals interact, communicate, and shape social realities. With each advancement, novel behavioural patterns arise, existing power structures are either contested or upheld, and the essence of social interaction undergoes transformation. Sociologists must examine how media functions as both a mirror of society and a catalyst for social change, especially within the framework of the digital revolution.

Historical Context of Media Technologies and Societal Transformation

The influence of media technology on society can be perceived as a cumulative process that evolves from previous innovations. The printing press revolutionised information access by increasing the availability of written texts, thereby enhancing literacy and disseminating Enlightenment ideas that instigated democratic revolutions in Europe. By facilitating independent access to information, it undermined religious and monarchical authority over knowledge and established a basis for a more informed and engaged populace.

Sociologists have observed that subsequent technological advancements further broadened the democratisation of information, each carrying distinct sociocultural implications. The advent of radio and television facilitated the simultaneous transmission of messages to a wider, more diverse audience, fostering a shared experience and a collective consciousness regarding significant events. This mass media model—where a limited number of producers disseminated information to millions of recipients—established media as a significant institution in society, capable of influencing norms, political perspectives, and cultural values.

The Digital Revolution and Media Convergence

The shift from traditional to digital media signifies a fundamental change in content production and consumption, as well as in societal structure. The phenomenon of media convergence, in which various media forms amalgamate on digital platforms, has transformed the accessibility and dissemination of information. Digital platforms such as social media, news websites, and streaming services facilitate the integration of textual, visual, and interactive content. This transition blurs the previously distinct boundaries between producers and consumers, as audiences now engage actively in content creation and distribution.

Media convergence has led to what sociologists term a "participatory culture," wherein the distinction between audience and creator is obscured. Social media platforms such as YouTube, Instagram, and TikTok enable individuals to act as "prosumers" (simultaneous producers and consumers of media), thereby influencing and curating public discourse. Nonetheless, this participation frequently exhibits disparity, as algorithmic platforms favour content that enhances engagement. This influences the nature of information disseminated to the public and moulds public discourse by favouring sensational, emotionally charged content over nuanced, fact-based information. Consequently, technology amplifies specific voices and viewpoints while marginalising others, thereby reinforcing social hierarchies and biases.

The Information Ecosystem: Velocity, Accessibility, and Disinformation

The rapidity and accessibility of digital media signify a significant societal transformation. The internet has facilitated instantaneous communication and the swift distribution of information, establishing a global "information ecosystem" in which news, ideas, and cultural symbols circulate freely and rapidly. This transition is advantageous for many, as it democratises information and enhances global awareness. However, the extensive amount of accessible content can inundate individuals, resulting in "information fatigue" and diminished ability for critical engagement. Sociologists examining media consumption contend that this fosters a "culture of immediacy," wherein individuals prioritise the rapidity and novelty of information over its depth and accuracy.

This phenomenon is exacerbated by the ubiquity of misinformation and "fake news," which flourish in digital environments. Social media platforms prioritise content that generates substantial engagement, thereby inadvertently promoting sensational or misleading information that disseminates rapidly and extensively. Fabricated information has tangible societal repercussions, ranging from affecting electoral outcomes to provoking violence, as evidenced by numerous occurrences worldwide. In India, for instance, misinformation disseminated through WhatsApp has resulted in episodes of mob violence, demonstrating how the extensive reach of digital media can intensify social tensions. Sociologists associate this phenomenon with the concept of "moral panics," wherein media-induced hysteria engenders excessive public fear or outrage, frequently directed at particular groups or behaviours.

Algorithmic Content and the Fragmentation of Social Reality

A defining characteristic of digital media platforms is their dependence on algorithms that customise content for individual users based on historical behaviour, interactions, and preferences. This has rendered digital media more captivating, yet it has also resulted in the emergence of "filter bubbles" and "echo chambers," wherein individuals predominantly encounter information that corroborates their pre-existing convictions. From a sociological standpoint, this fosters the fragmentation of social reality, as individuals reside in separate "information silos" with minimal exposure to alternative perspectives. The outcome frequently manifests as increased political and ideological polarisation, as individuals cultivate disparate perceptions of reality influenced by the content they engage with.

This phenomenon is particularly pertinent in the realm of social and political life, where algorithmically generated content can affect public opinion and electoral behaviour. During elections, social media algorithms can disproportionately enhance specific narratives or candidates, influencing electoral results and democratic processes. Sociologists such as Jürgen Habermas have posited the significance of a "public sphere" wherein individuals can participate in rational discourse and deliberation. Nonetheless, the fragmentation induced by algorithm-driven content undermines this ideal, as individuals become increasingly ensconced within ideological bubbles, thereby diminishing opportunities for constructive dialogue and mutual comprehension.

Mobilisation of Social and Political Movements in the Digital Era

Notwithstanding its challenges, digital media has served as a potent instrument for social and political mobilisation, particularly for marginalised communities. Social media platforms have empowered activists to organise, advocate, and engage extensive audiences, frequently circumventing the gatekeeping of traditional media. Movements such as #MeToo, Black Lives Matter, and India's #JusticeForDalit illustrate how digital platforms enhance visibility for issues frequently neglected by mainstream media. The capabilities of digital media—such as sharing real-time information, organising protests, and disseminating awareness—facilitate collective action and promote solidarity across geographic boundaries.

Nonetheless, the digital mobilisation model has resulted in the occurrence of "slacktivism," wherein individuals endorse causes online without substantial involvement or action. Sociologists contend that although digital activism enhances visibility, it may also undermine the efficacy of movements by fostering a misleading perception of participation. Furthermore, digital activism is susceptible to state and corporate surveillance, which may compromise its effectiveness. Governments and corporations surveil and suppress online dissent via censorship or data collection, undermining the concept of the internet as an intrinsically "democratic" environment.

Economic Transformations: The Gig Economy and Consumer Conduct

The proliferation of digital platforms has altered economic frameworks, facilitating the rise of the gig economy and modifying consumer behaviour. Digital platforms such as Uber, Swiggy, and Upwork have established a new category of "gig workers," who engage in freelance or temporary employment devoid of the security and benefits linked to conventional jobs. Sociologists examining labour contend that although the gig economy provides flexibility, it simultaneously heightens economic precarity due to the absence of job stability and protections for workers. This transition signifies overarching trends in neoliberalism, wherein economic frameworks progressively emphasise profit at the expense of worker welfare.

Digital media has transformed consumer behaviour, fostering a culture of convenience and personalisation. The emergence of e-commerce platforms such as Amazon and Flipkart has expedited shopping and enhanced accessibility, fulfilling consumers' demand for immediate satisfaction. This has raised concerns regarding sustainability, as accelerated consumption patterns contribute to environmental degradation and exploitative labour practices. The sociological notion of "commodification" is pertinent, as an increasing number of life aspects are rendered marketable, prompting consumers to derive identity and fulfilment from material possessions.

Cultural Transformations and the Globalisation of Media

The digital age has expedited the globalisation of media, facilitating the intercultural exchange of ideas, values, and aesthetics. Sociologists indicate that although this fosters cultural diversity and comprehension, it simultaneously leads to cultural homogenisation, as Western media frequently predominates global content. This affects local cultures, particularly in areas with robust traditional values. In India, the prevalence of Westernised media has impacted fashion, language, and social norms, occasionally resulting in generational conflicts as younger audiences adopt globalised content.

The impact of global media prompts enquiries regarding cultural hegemony, wherein dominant nations mould global perceptions and values via media. Stuart Hall's theory of "encoding and decoding" is pertinent, as audiences interpret media messages through their cultural perspectives, occasionally resisting or reinterpreting prevailing narratives. This process illustrates the intricate interplay between global and local cultures in the digital era, wherein individuals interact with and reinterpret cultural significances in manners that both challenge and adhere to dominant ideals.

Sociological Consequences and the Prospects of Media

The continuous advancement of media and technology indicates that society will persist in experiencing significant changes. As digital platforms become more entwined with everyday life, concerns regarding data privacy, digital literacy, and regulation grow increasingly pressing. Sociologists underscore the significance of media literacy, especially as digital media emerges as a predominant source of information. A comprehensive understanding of media empowers individuals to traverse the intricacies of the digital realm, facilitating informed decision-making and resisting manipulation.

The future of media will be influenced by advancements in artificial intelligence, virtual reality, and other emerging technologies, potentially redefining human interaction and societal norms. These technologies possess the capacity to exacerbate existing inequalities or cultivate novel avenues of connection and comprehension. The intersection of technology and media necessitates sociological inquiry to comprehend their effects on social structures, relationships, and cultural values. The relationship among media, society, and technology is reciprocal, with each influencing and being influenced by the others in intricate and frequently unpredictable manners.

An Overview of Media in India

The media landscape in India is extensive, varied, and evolving, influenced by historical contexts and contemporary technological progress. The media in India has consistently wielded significant influence in societal transformation, from its involvement in the independence movement to its current function as a guardian of democracy. The origins of Indian media can be traced to the colonial era, during which the press functioned as an essential instrument for freedom fighters to express dissent against British governance. Newspapers, especially regional publications, served as venues for political and social discourse, cultivating a sense of national identity. Following independence, the inception of All India Radio (AIR) and Doordarshan signified the commencement of government-regulated media in India. For decades, these served as the principal sources of news and entertainment, influencing collective narratives and fostering national unity.

The liberalisation of the 1990s facilitated the entry of private entities into the media sector, resulting in increased diversity and competition. Currently, India possesses a robust media ecosystem that includes television, radio, print, and digital platforms. This diversity exemplifies India's linguistic and cultural wealth, as regional media serves local audiences in vernacular languages. In regions such as Tamil Nadu, West Bengal, and Maharashtra, local newspapers and television channels continue to thrive, offering coverage that is more pertinent to regional issues and concerns. The proliferation of digital media has broadened this landscape, with internet access extending to rural regions and facilitating access to both global and hyper-local content.

Nonetheless, the Indian media landscape faces numerous challenges. Concentration of ownership is a critical issue, as substantial business conglomerates dominate major media outlets, raising concerns regarding editorial autonomy. Political pressures, censorship, and self-regulation introduce complexities, especially for journalists aiming to cover sensitive topics. The proliferation of misinformation, particularly on digital platforms, presents a novel challenge to credibility and public trust. Nevertheless, despite these obstacles, Indian media remains pivotal in fostering social awareness and education, providing varied content that informs, entertains, and occasionally contests societal norms.

Transformations in Power Dynamics: The Influence of Politics on Media

The interplay between media and politics is characterised by reciprocal influence and shifting power dynamics. Media serves as a fundamental institution in democratic societies, theoretically functioning as the "fourth estate" by holding power accountable, fostering public discourse, and ensuring governmental transparency. The interaction between politics and media frequently obscures this idealised role, as political figures endeavour to influence media narratives while media outlets often align with particular political agendas. This dynamic significantly influences how citizens in India and worldwide perceive reality, develop opinions, and engage in the political process. The evolving power dynamics in this relationship prompt sociological enquiries regarding media ownership, freedom of expression, and the influence of technology in either reinforcing or contesting political authority.

Media as an Instrument of Political Authority

Historically, political leaders and governments have acknowledged the capacity of media to influence public opinion. In India, this influence originates from the independence movement, during which newspapers such as *Kesari* and *Young India* functioned as platforms for anti-colonial discourse. These publications galvanised support for independence by disseminating nationalist ideas, fostering a collective identity among Indians, and inciting action against British rule. In this context, media was perceived as an instrument of resistance, granting a voice to individuals contesting colonial power structures.

Following independence, the Indian government promptly sought to regulate mass media to foster a unified national identity. State-operated media outlets such as All India Radio (AIR) and Doordarshan were created to foster national unity, development, and cultural identity. This stringent regulation resulted in media frequently mirroring the government's perspective, a phenomenon noted worldwide in newly independent nations striving for stability and legitimacy. Although AIR and Doordarshan significantly contributed to informing citizens and cultivating a sense of national identity, critics contend that state control restricted dissent and critical discourse regarding government policies.

The liberalisation of India's economy in the 1990s resulted in diversified media ownership, facilitating the rise of private news channels and a competitive media landscape. This facilitated increased diversity and independent viewpoints, but also brought in commercial interests and vulnerability to political influence. Sociologists note that the interaction between media and political power becomes increasingly intricate in capitalist societies, where profit motives and corporate ownership influence media narratives. Currently, numerous media organisations in India are owned by substantial conglomerates with connections to political figures, thereby affecting editorial content and reporting methodologies. This affects journalistic independence, as media organisations may engage in self-censorship or present news narratives that conform to the interests of owners or advertisers, who frequently possess political affiliations.

Political Bias and Media Fragmentation

In democratic societies, the media ideally provides a variety of viewpoints, enabling citizens to develop informed opinions. Nonetheless, media bias—both explicit and implicit—has progressively influenced public perception. Political parties acknowledge media as a means for advancing specific ideologies, resulting in the occurrence of "partisan media," in which news outlets affiliate with distinct political agendas. In India, this alignment is manifest as numerous news channels and newspapers either implicitly or explicitly endorse political parties, especially during electoral periods.

From a sociological standpoint, this partisanship engenders a "media echo chamber" effect, wherein audiences are primarily exposed to information that corroborates their pre-existing convictions. This segmentation of media audiences results in ideological polarisation, wherein individuals engaging with disparate media sources possess divergent, frequently conflicting, interpretations of reality. Sociologists posit that this polarisation undermines democratic discourse by diminishing common ground and fostering social division. In India, media biases can shape public opinion on contentious issues such as religion, caste, and nationalism, exacerbating social divisions and hindering constructive discourse.

The sociologist Jürgen Habermas's notion of the "public sphere" elucidates the ramifications of this polarisation. In an optimal public sphere, citizens participate in rational and inclusive discourse regarding societal issues, culminating in consensus and collective decision-making. The segmentation of media audiences and the dominance of politically motivated reporting undermine this ideal, substituting rational discourse with sensationalism and ideological echo chambers. In this context, political parties utilise media as a platform for divisive rhetoric, which can undermine meaningful policy discussions and diminish democratic engagement to a competition of identities and affiliations.

Media Proprietorship, Corporate Interests, and Political Influence

The consolidation of media ownership within a limited number of influential conglomerates has profound implications for the media's function in democratic societies. Media corporations frequently maintain financial connections to political entities, whether through direct ownership, advertising revenue, or corporate interests aligned with particular policies. The concentration of ownership limits the diversity of viewpoints available to the public, as editorial content mirrors the interests of media proprietors and advertisers. In India, prominent media networks such as Zed News and Times Group are integrated within larger conglomerates that possess diverse business interests, including sectors reliant on advantageous government policies.

Corporate ownership may result in nuanced censorship, wherein journalists and editors engage in self-censorship to evade subjects that could threaten their employers' interests. For example, investigative journalism concerning corporate malfeasance or environmental degradation by significant corporations may be minimised or overlooked by media organisations owned by those same entities. This undermines the watchdog function of journalism, jeopardising the media's role as an institution that ensures accountability of power. Furthermore, the reliance of media on advertising revenue incentivises the prioritisation of content that garners viewership over content that is inherently informative or investigative. This results in sensationalism and infotainment, frequently compromising critical journalism.

The impact of political advertising exacerbates this relationship. Political parties and candidates allocate substantial resources to media campaigns, particularly during elections, establishing financial dependencies between media organisations and political entities. This phenomenon is especially evident on television channels and digital platforms, where political advertisements can monopolise airtime, influencing public opinion and electoral behaviour. The distinction between journalism and political advocacy becomes indistinct, eroding public confidence in media as an unbiased information source.

The Influence of Social Media on Political Discourse

The emergence of social media has undermined conventional power hierarchies in media and altered the dynamics of the relationship between politics and media. Social media platforms, including Facebook, Twitter, and Instagram, facilitate direct communication between politicians and citizens, circumventing conventional media gatekeepers. This transition enables political figures to manage their narratives, galvanise supporters, and react to events instantaneously. In India, Prime Minister Narendra Modi's social media presence illustrates this phenomenon, as his posts instantly reach millions of followers, bypassing journalistic scrutiny.

Although social media has democratised access to political information, it has concurrently enabled the dissemination of misinformation and propaganda. The algorithmic structure of social media platforms promotes content that achieves significant engagement, frequently prioritising sensational or polarising material over factual reporting. Political actors manipulate these algorithms to propagate divisive narratives, cultivating "us vs. them" mentalities that exacerbate social divisions. In India, platforms such as WhatsApp have disseminated misinformation during elections, impacting voter behaviour and exacerbating communal tensions. Sociologists associate this phenomenon with the concept of "moral panic," wherein media-induced fears regarding specific groups or issues generate increased public anxiety, frequently advantageous to political figures who exploit these concerns.

Furthermore, the absence of regulation on social media has facilitated "astroturfing," wherein fabricated grassroots movements are orchestrated to create the illusion of extensive public endorsement for a political agenda. This influences public perception, as individuals may perceive certain opinions as more prevalent or credible than they actually are. Social media has facilitated the emergence of "troll armies," wherein coordinated factions perpetrate harassment or disinformation campaigns against political adversaries, journalists, and activists, engendering a climate of fear that suppresses free expression.

Obstacles to Press Freedom and Journalistic Autonomy

In democratic societies, the freedom of the press is crucial for accountability and transparency. Nonetheless, political pressures on media organisations and journalists compromise this liberty. In India, journalists covering corruption, communal violence, or human rights violations frequently encounter harassment, legal obstacles, or even physical violence. The suppression of dissent hinders the dissemination of information to the public, thereby constraining the ability for informed democratic engagement. The proliferation of defamation lawsuits and the application of sedition laws against journalists and activists adversely impact press freedom, discouraging critical reporting and fostering self-censorship.

The heightened politicisation of regulatory agencies raises apprehensions regarding media autonomy. The Indian government's influence over entities such as the Press Council of India and the Central Board of Film Certification impacts content production and distribution. Media organisations may engage in self-regulation to avert penalties or suspension, thereby influencing the nature of content accessible to the public. Sociologists contend that such censorship undermines the public sphere, as citizens are deprived of varied viewpoints on matters of national significance.

Technology as a Dual-Edged Instrument in Media-Politics Interactions

Although digital technology has enhanced media's ability to reach and engage the public, it also presents challenges to democratic discourse. The utilisation of big data and artificial intelligence in political campaigns facilitates targeted messaging, enabling candidates to present customised content to particular demographics. This micro-targeting can influence voter behaviour by leveraging individuals' personal data and psychological profiles, frequently without their informed consent. The Cambridge Analytica scandal illustrates the ethical issues surrounding data privacy and the exploitation of personal information for political advantage.

Artificial intelligence and machine learning facilitate the production of "deepfakes"—altered videos and images that generate realistic yet deceptive representations of public figures. Deepfakes pose a threat to democracy by facilitating the dissemination of disinformation, undermining reputations, and potentially inciting violence. With technological advancements, these tools may become more accessible, thereby complicating the verification of information and the accountability of political actors.

Advancing Critical Media Literacy

The evolving power relations between media and politics highlight the necessity for critical media literacy within society. Sociologists contend that promoting media literacy enables citizens to discern biases, identify disinformation, and critically engage with media content. In India, where political influence on media is significant, media literacy is essential for democratic resilience. Educational initiatives that instruct citizens in critical media analysis, propaganda recognition, and accountability demand can enhance the media's function as a platform for democratic engagement rather than as an instrument of political manipulation.

As the distinctions among media, technology, and politics increasingly converge, comprehending the sociological ramifications of this interplay is crucial. The power dynamics that shape media and politics are not fixed; they develop in response to technological progress, regulatory modifications, and changing social conventions. Through sociological analysis of these changes, citizens and policymakers can cultivate a media landscape that upholds democratic principles and fosters a more informed and engaged populace.

CHAPTER II

KEY IDEAS IN MEDIA STUDIES

The sociology of media is a rich and dynamic field that examines the intricate relationships between media, society, and culture. As media technologies evolve and proliferate, they reshape not only how information is disseminated but also how individuals and communities construct their identities, understand social realities, and engage with one another. This section aims to explore key ideas and theories that form the foundation of sociological analysis of media, drawing on seminal contributions from influential thinkers.

At the core of this field lies the understanding that media are not neutral channels of communication; rather, they are active agents that shape social relations and power dynamics. Theories originating from Marxist thought provide a critical lens through which to analyse how media operate within capitalist frameworks, reinforcing existing power structures and ideologies. Scholars like Antonio Gramsci and Louis Althusser expand upon Marxist ideas by emphasizing concepts such as hegemony and ideological state apparatuses, which illuminate how consent and ideological alignment are maintained in society.

Meanwhile, the Frankfurt School introduces a critical theory perspective, critiquing the mass media's role in promoting consumerism and conformity through the culture industry. Their work underscores the media's potential to shape public consciousness and societal values, often in ways that inhibit critical thought and meaningful engagement.

As we move into the realm of media technologies, theorists such as Marshall McLuhan and Brian Winston provide insights into how the very form of media influences human perception and social interaction. McLuhan's assertion that "the medium is the message" challenges us to consider the profound effects of media technologies beyond their content, while Winston's analysis of the suppression of radical potential highlights the socio-economic forces that shape the development and adoption of new media.

Finally, the postmodern turn in media studies invites us to examine the fragmented and contradictory nature of contemporary media culture, as articulated by thinkers like Jean Baudrillard and Roland Barthes. Concepts such as simulacra, hyperreality, and the death of the author encourage a deeper understanding of how media texts create meaning and how audiences actively interpret and engage with these texts.

This section will delve into these foundational theories and concepts, exploring how they intersect and inform our understanding of the media's role in shaping social life. Through this exploration, we aim to provide a comprehensive overview of the key ideas in the sociology of media, equipping readers with the analytical tools necessary to critically engage with the media landscape in an increasingly complex and interconnected world.

MARXISM AND MEDIA

Marxism is a social, political, and economic theory originated by Karl Marx, which focuses on the struggle between capitalists and the working class. In media studies, Marxist theory is used to analyse how the media operate within capitalist societies and contribute to the maintenance of the status quo.

Base and Superstructure

The concept of "base and superstructure" is a foundational idea in Marxist theory, shaping how we understand the relationship between economic forces and societal institutions. According to Marx, society is structured into two primary components: the economic "base" and the ideological "superstructure." This model asserts that the base, comprising the means and relations of production (such as Labour, capital, and ownership), shapes and sustains the superstructure, which includes institutions like media, education, law, and religion. The superstructure, in turn, reflects the interests and values of those who control the base—in most societies, the capitalist class. By examining media as part of the superstructure, Marxist theorists analyse how media reflects and reinforces the ideologies and interests of those who own and control the means of production.

The base encompasses all economic elements that form the foundation of a society. This includes the productive forces, such as technology, resources, and Labour, as well as the relations of production, which determine how wealth and resources are distributed. The relations of production refer to the roles and relationships between various classes, such as owners and workers, within the economic system. Marx argued that the structure of these relationships directly impacts the rest of society, including its values, norms, and belief systems.

The superstructure, on the other hand, comprises the institutions and cultural phenomena that are built upon this economic base. The media, as part of the superstructure, plays a significant role in propagating and normalizing the ideologies that serve the interests of the ruling capitalist class. In a capitalist society, the base—controlled by those who own capital—creates conditions that influence the superstructure. Media institutions, which require significant capital to operate, are thus beholden to those who own the means of production. Through content, they promote ideologies that maintain the status quo and discourage alternative economic or social systems.

Historically, this relationship can be observed in shifts in media technology and ownership, reflecting changes in the economic base. In the early 20th century, newspapers were the dominant media form, and their ownership was concentrated among wealthy capitalists. This concentration allowed owners to influence public opinion in ways that aligned with their interests, such as promoting free-market ideologies or opposing labour unions. As media evolved to include radio, television, and, eventually, digital platforms, ownership remained concentrated, with large corporations and wealthy individuals controlling most mainstream media. This economic base influences the superstructure by limiting the diversity of viewpoints and creating content that favours capitalist ideologies.

In practical terms, the base-superstructure model suggests that media narratives often reflect the interests of the capitalist class. This can be observed in the types of stories that are prioritized, the way issues are framed, and the voices that are amplified or marginalized. For example, news coverage often emphasizes stories that promote consumerism, individualism, and competition—values that are integral to a capitalist economy. Success stories of entrepreneurs and self-made millionaires are highlighted, while systemic issues like poverty and inequality are frequently overlooked or framed as personal failures. This creates a narrative that reinforces the idea that success is achievable for anyone within the capitalist system, obscuring the structural barriers that limit opportunities for the working class.

One critique of the base-superstructure model is that it can be overly deterministic, suggesting that the superstructure is simply a reflection of the base with little autonomy. Scholars like Raymond Williams have argued that the relationship between base and superstructure is more complex and dynamic. Williams proposed that cultural institutions have some degree of autonomy and can influence the base in certain contexts. For example, media institutions may sometimes challenge the capitalist system by promoting social justice issues or giving voice to marginalized groups. However, even these counter-hegemonic narratives are often limited by economic constraints, such as advertising revenue and market demands, which ultimately tie them back to the base.

In media studies, the base-superstructure model provides a valuable framework for understanding how economic interests shape media content. By analysing who owns and controls media institutions,

Marxist theorists can identify the ways in which media content supports capitalist ideologies. For instance, large media conglomerates, driven by profit motives, may prioritize sensationalist stories that attract viewers and advertisers over in-depth reporting on systemic issues. This focus on profit over public service illustrates how the economic base influences the superstructure.

The base-superstructure model also highlights the role of media in legitimizing the capitalist system. By presenting capitalist values as natural and inevitable, media contribute to what Marx called "false consciousness," where people accept their social conditions without questioning the underlying power dynamics. This ideological function of media is crucial for maintaining the stability of the capitalist system, as it discourages collective action and resistance by framing individual success as the primary path to fulfilment.

In conclusion, the base-superstructure model is a central concept in Marxist media theory, illustrating how economic forces shape cultural institutions and ideologies. By examining media as part of the superstructure, Marxist theorists reveal how media content reflects the interests of the capitalist class, promoting ideologies that sustain the existing social order. While the model has its limitations, it remains a powerful tool for analysing the relationship between economic power and cultural production in capitalist societies. Through this lens, we can better understand how media serves as a vehicle for capitalist ideologies, subtly shaping public consciousness and reinforcing the structures of power that define our society.

Ideology

In Marxist theory, the concept of "ideology" is crucial for understanding how societies function and why people often accept the social systems in which they live. Marxist ideology refers to a set of beliefs, ideas, and values that reflect the interests of the ruling class, the group that controls society's economic base. Ideology is not simply a collection of random beliefs but rather a structured worldview that makes the status quo—how things are now—seem natural and inevitable. Media, in particular, play a central role in promoting and reinforcing this worldview.

Understanding Ideology in Marxist Terms

Karl Marx and Friedrich Engels first introduced the concept of ideology in *The German Ideology* (1846), where they argued that the ruling ideas of any age are the ideas of the ruling class. In simpler terms, the beliefs and values that dominate society often serve the interests of those in power. The media, as part of the ideological "superstructure," become a powerful tool for spreading these ideas widely. When people internalize these beliefs, they tend to accept the current social system without questioning it, which helps maintain the power of the ruling class.

For example, consider the common belief that "hard work leads to success." In many capitalist societies, this idea is widespread, encouraging people to work hard with the expectation of personal rewards, such as wealth or status. While hard work is undoubtedly valuable, this belief can mask the economic inequalities that exist in society. Not everyone has the same opportunities, and systemic barriers like class, race, and gender can affect a person's ability to succeed. By focusing on individual effort and merit, this ideology downplays the structural obstacles that many people face and makes economic inequality seem like a result of personal failure rather than an issue with the social system itself.

The Media as an Ideological Tool

Media serve as a primary vehicle for promoting these ideologies. Whether it's through news programs, films, advertisements, or even social media, the content we consume influences our ideas about the world. In a capitalist society, where profit and private ownership are key, media often promote values that align with capitalism, such as individualism, consumerism, and competition. These values are not random but reflect the interests of the ruling class, who benefit from a society where people aspire to wealth and success.

For instance, advertisements often promote the idea that happiness and success come from buying products. This focus on consumerism encourages people to work harder to afford more goods, reinforcing the capitalist cycle of production and consumption. Similarly, news programs may prioritize stories about successful entrepreneurs, subtly promoting the idea that wealth is achievable for anyone with enough effort. This can create a "common sense" understanding of society, where people see capitalism as a natural and even desirable system.

Case Study: The American Dream

One well-known example of ideology in media is the concept of the "American Dream," which is especially prevalent in the United States. The American Dream suggests that anyone, regardless of background, can achieve success and prosperity through hard work. This idea is widely promoted in American media, from movies that celebrate rags-to-riches stories to news stories that highlight individual achievements. The American Dream aligns with capitalist values by promoting individual success and financial achievement as ultimate life goals.

However, this narrative can obscure social inequalities by suggesting that people are solely responsible for their own success or failure. Structural issues like limited access to education, healthcare, or a living wage are often left out of the story. As a result, the American Dream can reinforce the belief that poverty or failure results from individual shortcomings, not from systemic problems. By promoting this ideology, media help maintain the capitalist system by discouraging people from challenging the inequalities embedded within it.

How Ideology Works Subtly

Ideology in media does not often appear as blatant propaganda; it's usually subtle and works through repetition. When people are exposed to certain ideas repeatedly over time, they begin to internalize them. For example, if media consistently show successful businesspeople as heroes, this creates an association between success and individualism, making capitalism appear as the best, most natural economic system.

French philosopher Louis Althusser expanded on Marx's ideas, arguing that institutions like media act as "ideological state apparatuses." This means they work alongside other institutions (like schools and churches) to reinforce beliefs that align with the ruling class's interests. Althusser noted that media don't need to use force to control people; by shaping people's ideas, they gain consent to the existing social structure. This process helps explain why people often accept social conditions without question.

Critiques of Ideology in Media

Critics argue that the Marxist view of ideology can sometimes be too simplistic, suggesting that people are passively accepting whatever the media presents. Audience studies, particularly those from Cultural Studies scholars, show that people often interpret media in complex ways, sometimes resisting dominant ideologies. For instance, not everyone who watches a film about wealth internalizes capitalist values; some may critique or reject the film's message.

Yet, even with these critiques, the concept of ideology remains useful for understanding how media can shape social beliefs and norms. The media's focus on consumerism, individualism, and the American Dream, for example, reveals how deeply ingrained capitalist ideologies are in society.

3. Hegemony (Gramsci)

The concept of hegemony is central to understanding how societies maintain power structures, especially when it comes to media's influence on culture and belief systems. Developed by Italian Marxist philosopher Antonio Gramsci, hegemony describes a process through which the ruling class maintains control, not merely through force but through a more subtle form of influence and consent. In other words, rather than relying on military or police power to enforce dominance, the ruling class achieves consent from the population by shaping cultural values, beliefs, and common sense ideas. Media play a critical role in establishing and reinforcing this consensual control, helping to keep existing social hierarchies in place by creating an understanding of the world that aligns with the ruling class's interests.

What is Hegemony?

In Marxist terms, hegemony is a process that allows the ruling class to maintain power through cultural and ideological means rather than overt force. Gramsci expanded on Marx's original ideas by explaining that for a ruling class to effectively control society, it must win the consent of the majority, even if this majority is oppressed or exploited within the system. Hegemony is achieved when the values and norms of the ruling class become the "common sense" values of the entire society. This process happens gradually, as ideas, beliefs, and social practices that benefit the ruling class are integrated into everyday life and accepted as natural or inevitable.

One way to understand hegemony is to think about how certain ideas come to seem "normal" or "common sense." These ideas are not neutral; they often support the interests of those in power. For instance, the idea that a capitalist economy is the best or only viable system becomes normalized through repeated exposure in the media, education, and cultural institutions. Over time, people come to accept capitalism as the natural order of things, even if it may not benefit them personally. This widespread acceptance helps maintain the dominance of the capitalist class without direct oppression.

Media's Role in Creating Hegemony

The media are one of the primary tools through which hegemony is established and maintained. Through news, entertainment, advertisements, and social media, the media shape the way people perceive reality. They do this by promoting certain values and ideas that align with the interests of the ruling class, such as consumerism, individualism, and competition. By framing these values as "common sense," media create a worldview that seems natural and unquestionable, discouraging people from considering alternative systems or questioning existing inequalities.

For example, in a capitalist society, the media often highlight individual success stories that reinforce the idea of "meritocracy"—the belief that people succeed based on talent and effort alone. Stories of entrepreneurs or self-made millionaires are celebrated, while the structural barriers that make it difficult for most people to achieve such success are rarely discussed. By emphasizing individual responsibility and success, the media reinforce the idea that anyone can succeed if they work hard enough, which diverts attention from systemic issues like class inequality, lack of access to resources, or discriminatory practices.

Gramsci's Idea of "Common Sense"

A key part of Gramsci's theory is the idea of "common sense," which refers to the everyday beliefs and values people hold that seem self-evident or natural. Common sense is not based on critical thinking or analysis but is a collection of ideas people accept as true because they are constantly reinforced by media, education, family, and other cultural institutions. In this way, common sense can serve as a vehicle for hegemonic control because it allows the ruling class to embed their interests within the fabric of everyday life.

For example, the media might portray consumerism as a natural and desirable way of life. Advertisements, movies, and TV shows often promote the idea that buying goods brings happiness and fulfillment. Over time, this focus on consumerism becomes part of "common sense," shaping people's understanding of happiness and success. By promoting consumerism, the media reinforce a cycle of consumption that supports the capitalist economy and benefits the ruling class.

Examples of Hegemony in Media

Media often present a particular view of the world that aligns with the interests of the ruling class. For instance, news coverage of social issues may focus on crime as an individual moral failing rather than discussing broader social causes like poverty or lack of education. This perspective diverts attention from systemic issues and keeps people from questioning the social structure itself.

Another example is the portrayal of "the American Dream" in U.S. media. The American Dream, which suggests that anyone can achieve success through hard work, aligns with capitalist values and reinforces the idea that social mobility is within everyone's reach. However, this narrative often ignores structural factors that limit opportunities for many people, such as economic inequality or racial discrimination. By framing success as an individual achievement, the media reinforce the capitalist system without directly addressing its inequalities.

Critiques and Limitations of Hegemony

While Gramsci's concept of hegemony has been widely influential, some critics argue that it can be too deterministic, suggesting that people passively accept whatever ideas the ruling class promotes. In reality, people have agency, and they do not always accept dominant ideologies without question. Studies in media and cultural studies have shown that audiences can interpret and even resist media messages in various ways, creating their own meanings from the content they consume. For example, people may watch a film that promotes capitalist values but interpret it in a way that challenges or critiques those values.

Additionally, hegemony is not always stable. Gramsci himself noted that hegemony must be constantly maintained and is always subject to challenge. Counter-hegemonic movements, such as social justice movements, use media to promote alternative ideas and values, seeking to challenge the dominant worldview. For instance, independent news outlets and activist groups often use social media to raise awareness about social inequalities and encourage critical thinking about the status quo.

False Consciousness

In Marxist theory, the concept of false consciousness refers to a condition in which people are unable to recognize the real nature of their social and economic situation. In this state, individuals accept and even defend beliefs that actually work against their own interests, especially those of the working class. Marx used this concept to explain why the working class often accepts the capitalist system, even though it perpetuates exploitation and inequality. Media, as part of the superstructure, are seen as central in creating and sustaining false consciousness, shaping public perceptions in ways that prevent people from recognizing their own oppression.

Defining False Consciousness

The term "false consciousness" describes the phenomenon where people believe in ideas or ideologies that serve the interests of the ruling class rather than their own. This condition is not simply a lack of knowledge but a deeply ingrained misunderstanding of one's position within society and the forces that shape it. In a capitalist society, false consciousness helps maintain the social order by making economic inequalities appear normal, natural, or even beneficial. When individuals buy into the dominant ideology, they are less likely to challenge or resist the system, which stabilizes the power of the ruling class.

For example, a worker might believe that low wages are justified because they have not "worked hard enough" to earn more. This belief shifts responsibility from the economic system, which sets wages based on profit, to the individual, creating a sense of personal failure. In reality, the system itself may prevent the worker from earning a higher wage. False consciousness, then, obscures the real cause of economic hardships, making them seem like individual issues rather than structural problems.

The Role of Media in Creating False Consciousness

Media play a major role in creating and sustaining false consciousness by presenting a reality that reflects the interests of the ruling class. Through news, entertainment, advertisements, and other forms of content, the media can shape how people understand their social world. By focusing on individual achievements, consumer choices, and personal responsibility, media create an understanding of society that aligns with capitalist ideology. This approach diverts attention from the systemic nature of inequality, encouraging people to see themselves as individually responsible for their successes or failures.

For instance, television shows, movies, and social media influencers often promote consumerist lifestyles as symbols of success. When media glorify wealth, luxury, and individualism, they implicitly suggest that achieving happiness and fulfillment comes from personal consumption and material wealth. People are encouraged to believe that happiness is attainable through acquiring goods and status, which benefits the capitalist economy but does little to address or change the structural inequalities that affect their lives.

In addition, media often present work and career success as the primary measure of personal worth. Stories of "rags-to-riches" entrepreneurs, for example, are celebrated in the media, reinforcing the idea that anyone can achieve wealth and success with enough hard work. However, these narratives ignore the structural barriers that limit opportunities for most people, such as access to education, social networks, or resources. By focusing on individual success stories, the media create a distorted view of reality that masks the broader economic forces at play.

Reinforcing False Consciousness through News and Entertainment

False consciousness is also reinforced through news and entertainment that frame social issues in ways that obscure their root causes. News coverage, for example, may focus on crime as a problem of individual morality rather than as a symptom of poverty, lack of opportunity, or systemic inequality. This framing encourages people to view social issues as the result of individual failings, rather than as consequences of an unequal social system.

Reality television and celebrity culture further reinforce false consciousness by creating a fantasy world where wealth and fame are portrayed as achievable for anyone. Shows like "Keeping Up with the Kardashians" or talent competitions like "America's Got Talent" promote the idea that anyone can become rich and famous, diverting attention from the social and economic realities that prevent most people from reaching such heights. By glorifying individual success, these shows create a sense of false hope, where viewers believe that they, too, can achieve wealth and status if they work hard enough, even though the system itself may prevent them from doing so.

The Consequences of False Consciousness

False consciousness has significant implications for social and political life because it reduces the likelihood of collective action or resistance against the system. When individuals believe that their hardships are personal rather than structural, they are less likely to unite with others who face similar struggles. This lack of awareness prevents the working class from recognizing its collective power and taking action to address systemic injustices.

For example, if workers believe that their low wages are a result of personal failure or lack of skill, they are less likely to join unions or advocate for higher wages. Instead, they may internalize feelings of inadequacy, blaming themselves rather than the economic system. This self-blame reinforces the capitalist structure by discouraging people from questioning or challenging the conditions that create inequality. False consciousness thus serves the interests of the ruling class by keeping the working class divided, disempowered, and less likely to demand social or economic reforms.

Critiques and Limitations of False Consciousness

Some critics argue that the concept of false consciousness can be too simplistic, assuming that people passively accept whatever ideology is presented to them. Cultural Studies scholars, for example, have shown that audiences interpret media in diverse ways and do not simply internalize dominant ideologies without question. People may resist or reinterpret media messages based on their own experiences, identities, and perspectives.

Moreover, the concept of false consciousness does not account for the complexities of identity and intersectionality. People's awareness of their social situation may be shaped by factors like race, gender, or ethnicity, which can lead to different interpretations of the same media content. For instance, a person of color in a low-wage job might be more likely to recognize the systemic nature of economic inequality than someone who has not experienced similar discrimination.

Conclusion

In summary, false consciousness is a concept in Marxist theory that explains why people may accept beliefs that work against their own interests, particularly in capitalist societies. The media contribute to false consciousness by presenting a distorted view of reality that emphasizes individual responsibility and success, obscuring the structural nature of inequality. Through representations of consumerism, individualism, and personal success, media create a worldview that aligns with the interests of the ruling class, maintaining the capitalist status quo. Although people have the capacity to resist these messages, false consciousness remains a powerful tool for stabilizing social hierarchies by discouraging people from recognizing or challenging the inequalities embedded within the system.

Analysing Media through a Marxist Lens

Using Marxist theory to analyse media involves examining how media operate within capitalist societies to uphold the interests of the ruling class. This approach seeks to understand how media ownership, content, and economic forces shape public consciousness, reinforce dominant ideologies, and ultimately support the status quo. By looking at who controls the media, what messages are presented, and how economic pressures influence content, we can see how media contribute to maintaining social and economic inequalities.

Ownership and Control of Media

A fundamental question in Marxist media analysis is who owns and controls the media? Ownership and control are crucial because they determine what kinds of information and perspectives are shared with the public. In capitalist societies, media ownership is often concentrated in the hands of a few large corporations, which Marxist theorists argue is not coincidental. These corporations are typically owned by members of the ruling class, who have a vested interest in maintaining the current system. As a result, the media content they produce and distribute reflects and reinforces their values and beliefs.

In the United States, for instance, major media outlets like Comcast, Disney, and News Corporation dominate the market. These conglomerates are highly profitable and rely on advertising revenue, which often influences the content they produce. Since they operate within a capitalist framework, these media corporations tend to avoid content that would challenge the capitalist system itself. Instead, they produce content that supports capitalist ideologies, such as individualism, consumerism, and competition, keeping their audience aligned with ideas that maintain the power of the ruling class.

Content Analysis: Examining Media Messages

Marxist media analysis also involves studying the content of media messages to identify underlying ideologies. By examining representations of social groups, events, and issues, we can uncover the implicit values and beliefs promoted by media. For instance, Marxist theorists might ask questions like: How are different social classes represented? Are working-class characters portrayed sympathetically or stereotypically? What kinds of narratives are prioritized, and which are excluded?

Consider how poverty and wealth are portrayed in popular media. Wealthy characters in movies and TV shows are often depicted as successful, attractive, and happy, while poorer characters may be shown as unhappy or unsuccessful. Such portrayals subtly promote the idea that wealth is the key to happiness and success, reinforcing the capitalist belief that economic achievement is the ultimate measure of personal worth. This focus on wealth and success obscures the structural factors that contribute to economic inequality, such as limited access to education, healthcare, or fair wages.

Moreover, news coverage can often reflect capitalist ideologies by framing issues in ways that support the status quo. For example, Labour strikes or protests may be portrayed as disruptive or harmful, rather than as legitimate responses to unfair working conditions. By framing workers' actions in a negative light, the media discourage people from supporting movements that challenge capitalist exploitation. In contrast, stories that celebrate wealthy entrepreneurs or highlight individual success reinforce the capitalist narrative that personal ambition is the primary path to success.

Political Economy of the Media

The political economy of the media approach examines how economic forces, such as advertising revenue and government regulation, shape media content and ownership. In capitalist societies, media organizations rely heavily on advertising as a primary source of revenue, which influences both the content they produce and the perspectives they promote. Advertisers are usually corporations with their own agendas, which often align with capitalist interests. As a result, media companies may avoid controversial topics or perspectives that could alienate advertisers or challenge the capitalist system.

For instance, a television network that relies on car manufacturers for advertising revenue might avoid airing stories about environmental issues related to the automobile industry. This self-censorship aligns media content with the interests of advertisers, shaping public perceptions in ways that benefit corporations and maintain the capitalist system. Media companies, therefore, prioritize content that aligns with the values of their advertisers, creating a kind of indirect control over information that the public receives.

In addition, media organizations often compete in a marketplace where success is measured by ratings, viewership, and profits. This competition pushes media companies to focus on sensational, entertaining, or commercial content that attracts audiences, rather than content that fosters critical thinking or promotes social justice. As a result, complex issues like economic inequality or corporate power are often simplified or ignored, leaving viewers with a limited understanding of the systemic forces at play in society.

The Commodification of Media Content

Marxist media analysis also addresses the commodification of media content, which means that media products are created and sold like any other consumer goods. Television shows, movies, and news programs are all commodities designed to generate profit. This commercialization affects both the form and content of media, often prioritizing profit over quality or social value. In a capitalist society, media companies focus on producing content that will attract the largest audience, as larger audiences increase advertising revenue.

For example, reality TV shows, which are often cheap to produce, have become a major genre because they attract large audiences and maximize profits. Although reality shows are popular, they rarely offer viewers meaningful engagement with real-world issues or encourage critical thought. Instead, they often promote consumerism, superficial values, and individualism, reflecting capitalist values while providing little room for audiences to question the social system.

Audience Interpretation and Resistance

It's important to note that, while media content may reinforce dominant ideologies, audiences are not passive recipients of these messages. People interpret media content in diverse ways, sometimes even resisting the intended messages. Audience studies have shown that viewers bring their own experiences, perspectives, and identities to the media they consume, which can lead to alternative interpretations. For instance, some viewers might watch a film that glorifies consumerism but interpret it as a critique of materialistic culture, demonstrating a critical awareness of capitalist ideology.

This resistance challenges the deterministic view that media content solely serves the ruling class. Nevertheless, even if people interpret media in various ways, the repetition of certain capitalist values—like consumerism, competition, and individualism—makes them appear natural or inevitable over time. For this reason, Marxist theorists argue that media still play a significant role in shaping society's "common sense" and maintaining the capitalist status quo.

ANTONIO GRAMSCI

Hegemony and the Role of Consent

Antonio Gramsci expanded on Karl Marx's ideas by introducing the concept of **hegemony**, which emphasizes the importance of cultural consent in maintaining the power of the ruling class. Unlike Marx, who focused on economic control as the primary tool for sustaining the status quo, Gramsci argued that the ruling class does not solely rely on force to maintain its dominance. Instead, it secures power by shaping the ideas, beliefs, and values of society in a way that appears natural and consensual. This process involves winning the "consent" of the working class by embedding dominant ideologies in everyday life, making them seem universally accepted and aligned with everyone's best interests. Gramsci's concept of hegemony highlights how social stability is not maintained by coercion alone but through subtle and pervasive forms of influence embedded in cultural and intellectual institutions, including the media.

In practical terms, hegemony means that the ruling class's ideas become the "common sense" of society, shaping how people interpret their experiences and view the world. For example, mainstream media outlets may portray capitalist values—such as individualism, competition, and consumerism—as normal and beneficial to all, even though they primarily serve the interests of the ruling class. By reinforcing these ideas, the media help to secure the consent of the working class, making the social order seem natural and inevitable.

Organic Intellectuals and the Media as an Ideological Battleground

Gramsci believed that each social class produces its own **organic intellectuals**—individuals who articulate and spread the values and interests of their class. Unlike traditional intellectuals, who are often disconnected from the experiences of the working class, organic intellectuals emerge directly from within the working class and are deeply connected to its struggles and values. In the context of media, organic intellectuals from different classes may use various platforms to challenge or reinforce the dominant ideology. The media thus become a battleground where competing ideologies are debated, resisted, or reinforced.

For example, alternative media outlets, such as independent news sites or social media channels, can serve as spaces for organic intellectuals from marginalized communities to voice their perspectives, challenge mainstream narratives, and counter the dominant ideology. These platforms allow the working class to resist hegemony by creating spaces for dissent, where alternative worldviews can be shared. However, Gramsci also recognized that dominant groups exert a strong influence on media, making it difficult for counter-ideologies to gain visibility. Thus, even as media provide a space for ideological contestation, they often privilege voices that align with the interests of the ruling class, making it challenging for alternative ideas to reach a broad audience.

The Importance of Civil Society in Maintaining Hegemony

Gramsci argued that **civil society**—the network of institutions that include schools, religious organizations, and media outlets—plays a critical role in maintaining hegemony. Civil society institutions do not exert coercive power directly but instead operate at the level of ideas and values, shaping people's beliefs in subtle ways. The media, as part of civil society, serve as a crucial instrument for promoting the values and ideologies of the ruling class. By shaping public opinion, the media help to secure the consent of society, reducing the need for the state to rely on direct coercion.

For instance, media portrayals of poverty, success, and class can influence how people understand social issues. If poverty is depicted as a result of individual failure rather than structural inequality, viewers may blame individuals for their economic status instead of questioning the system itself. This framing encourages the public to accept the existing social order as just, discouraging them from seeking structural change. Through such representations, the media contribute to the normalization of inequality, making social hierarchies appear legitimate and inevitable.

Gramsci's Legacy in Media and Cultural Studies

Gramsci's ideas have had a lasting impact on media and cultural studies, especially in the analysis of ideology, representation, and power. His concept of hegemony has provided scholars with a framework for understanding how media can promote dominant ideologies while still allowing room for resistance and alternative perspectives. Scholars in media studies often use Gramsci's concept of hegemony to explore how media messages align with the interests of the ruling class, as well as how marginalized voices use media to challenge the dominant ideology.

In conclusion, Antonio Gramsci's work offers valuable insights into the complex role of media in maintaining or challenging power structures. Through the concept of hegemony, Gramsci demonstrated that dominance is achieved not just through force but through consent, with media playing a key role in shaping public opinion. His ideas on organic intellectuals and civil society continue to inform discussions about the role of media in reinforcing or resisting the dominant ideology, making Gramsci an essential figure in Marxist media theory.

LOUIS ALTHUSSER

Ideological State Apparatuses (ISAs) and Repressive State Apparatuses (RSAs)

Louis Althusser, a French Marxist philosopher, built on Marx's ideas by proposing the concept of **Ideological State Apparatuses (ISAs)**, which are institutions that shape individuals' beliefs and values to align with the interests of the ruling class. Althusser distinguished ISAs from **Repressive State Apparatuses (RSAs)** like the police and military, which maintain control through force. While RSAs function to repress dissent directly, ISAs—such as schools, religious institutions, and media—achieve control by shaping people's ideologies. By instilling beliefs that support the dominant class, ISAs ensure that individuals accept the existing social order as natural and desirable.

The media serve as a powerful ISA because they continually reinforce dominant ideologies, such as the virtues of capitalism, individualism, and consumerism. Through news stories, advertisements, and entertainment, the media encourage viewers to adopt certain beliefs and values that ultimately support the capitalist system. By doing so, the media contribute to the process of **ideological reproduction**, ensuring that each new generation is socialized to accept the current social structure without question.

Interpellation: How Individuals Are "Hailed" by Ideology

One of Althusser's key contributions to Marxist theory is the concept of **interpellation**, which describes how individuals are "hailed" or addressed by ideology and come to see themselves as subjects within a particular social system. Interpellation is a process through which individuals internalize dominant ideologies and identify with roles and identities that align with the interests of the ruling class. The media play a significant role in interpellation by presenting specific images, values, and narratives that reinforce particular identities and social roles.

For example, a television advertisement that targets consumers with images of success, happiness, and fulfillment associated with luxury goods is an instance of interpellation. Viewers are subtly "hailed" by the ad's message, encouraging them to see themselves as consumers who can attain happiness through purchasing products. By accepting this identity, individuals contribute to the functioning of capitalism, even if it may not ultimately serve their interests. In this way, the media interpellate individuals into accepting roles that reinforce the social order.

The Role of Media in Ideological Reproduction

According to Althusser, the media play a crucial role in **ideological reproduction**—the process of maintaining and perpetuating dominant ideologies across generations. Through consistent exposure to particular messages, individuals internalize the values and beliefs of the ruling class. For instance, popular movies often portray individual success as the result of hard work and perseverance, reinforcing the capitalist ideology of meritocracy. By emphasizing individual achievement, the media obscure the structural inequalities that limit opportunities for many people, making it less likely that individuals will question the system.

In the news, media often frame social issues in ways that align with the interests of the ruling class. For instance, discussions about crime may focus on individual perpetrators rather than on the social conditions that contribute to crime, such as poverty and lack of access to resources. By framing issues in this way, the media encourage viewers to see social problems as individual failings rather than as symptoms of broader structural inequalities.

Critiques of Althusser's Theory

While Althusser's ideas have been influential, they have also faced criticism. Some scholars argue that his concept of interpellation presents individuals as overly passive, assuming that they automatically accept the ideologies presented to them. Critics suggest that people interpret media messages in diverse ways and may resist or reinterpret dominant ideologies based on their own experiences. Audience studies, for instance, have shown that viewers do not simply internalize media messages but actively negotiate their meanings.

Others argue that Althusser's focus on ISAs does not fully account for the agency of individuals in resisting or challenging dominant ideologies. Despite these critiques, Althusser's work has had a significant impact on media studies, particularly in understanding how media contribute to the ideological reproduction of capitalist values.

FRANKFURT SCHOOL

Critical Theory and the Culture Industry

The Frankfurt School, a group of Marxist thinkers that included Theodor Adorno, Max Horkheimer, and Walter Benjamin, developed **Critical Theory** as a response to the ways in which culture and media were used to maintain social control. The Frankfurt School theorists argued that mass media, in its pursuit of profit, produces a **culture industry** that standardizes cultural products, promoting passive consumption and discouraging critical thinking. Through films, television shows, advertisements, and music, the culture industry promotes conformity, making it difficult for individuals to resist the dominant ideology or imagine alternative ways of living.

The Culture Industry: Mass Production of Cultural Products

According to the Frankfurt School, the **culture industry** turns culture into a commodity, producing standardized cultural products that are designed to be easily consumed. Movies, music, and television shows are produced with the primary goal of generating profit, leading to a homogenization of content that prioritizes entertainment over critical thought. Adorno and Horkheimer argued that this standardization leads to a decline in the quality of culture, as artists and creators are pressured to produce work that is formulaic and easily marketable.

For example, many Hollywood movies follow predictable formulas, with familiar plot structures, character archetypes, and visual styles. These formulas make cultural products easy to consume, but they also limit the potential for innovation and critical engagement. The Frankfurt School argued that the culture industry's emphasis on uniformity and profitability encourages audiences to passively consume media without questioning its messages or assumptions, creating a kind of "false consciousness" that discourages people from seeing social inequalities or envisioning alternative social arrangements.

Media as a Tool for Social Control

The Frankfurt School theorists believed that the culture industry serves as a tool for **social control** by promoting ideologies that support the capitalist system. Media content often reinforces capitalist values, such as individualism, consumerism, and competition, encouraging people to prioritize personal success over collective welfare. This focus on individual achievement and material wealth aligns with the interests of the ruling class, as it discourages people from questioning the economic system or organizing for social change.

For example, advertisements often promote products as essential to happiness, self-worth, or social status, leading people to associate personal fulfillment with consumption. This emphasis on consumerism creates a cycle where individuals work to earn money so they can buy products that promise happiness, only to find that their sense of fulfillment is short-lived. By keeping people focused on consumption, the culture industry diverts attention away from systemic issues like economic inequality, environmental degradation, and social injustice.

Pseudo-Individualism and the Illusion of Choice

Adorno introduced the concept of **pseudo-individualism** to describe the illusion of choice within the culture industry. Although people may feel that they have a wide range of cultural products to choose from, these products are often variations on the same formulaic themes and ideas. For example, pop music may appear diverse, but many popular songs follow similar structures, lyrical themes, and production styles. This pseudo-individualism gives consumers the illusion of uniqueness, encouraging them to believe that they are making choices based on personal preference, when in reality, their options are limited by the dictates of the culture industry.

Critiques of the Frankfurt School

The Frankfurt School's views have been criticized for being overly pessimistic and for underestimating the agency of audiences. Critics argue that people are not simply passive consumers who uncritically accept media messages but are capable of interpreting and even resisting media in diverse ways. Audience studies have shown that people often bring their own experiences and perspectives to media, leading to varied interpretations and sometimes even subversive readings.
Furthermore, some scholars argue that the Frankfurt School's focus on standardization overlooks the diversity and creativity present in contemporary media. Independent films, alternative music scenes, and online media platforms offer spaces for innovative and critical content that challenges the mainstream. Despite these criticisms, the Frankfurt School's critique of the culture industry remains a valuable framework for understanding the relationship between media, culture, and ideology in capitalist societies.

Media Technologies and Power: Marshall McLuhan

Marshall McLuhan, a Canadian media theorist, is best known for his ideas about how media technologies impact society and culture. His work emphasizes that media technologies are not just channels for delivering content but are powerful forces that shape how people think, communicate, and experience the world. McLuhan's key concepts—"the medium is the message," hot and cool media, and the global village—each demonstrate his belief that the characteristics of a medium have profound effects on society.

The Medium is the Message

One of McLuhan's most famous ideas is the notion that "the medium is the message." This phrase implies that the nature of a medium itself, rather than its content, is the most significant factor influencing how people experience and interpret information. For McLuhan, the way media shape society depends on their form, which affects our senses and perceptions. He argued that each medium—be it print, television, or radio—alters human experience in a specific way. For instance, reading a book (a print medium) requires deep concentration and logical thought, engaging our visual sense in a unique way. On the other hand, television is a more immersive experience, combining visual and auditory stimulation to create an impact that differs entirely from print.

By suggesting that the medium itself influences human behaviour and society, McLuhan encourages us to look beyond the content of media and examine how different forms shape society at a deeper level. His insight remains relevant in today's digital age, where the forms of media, from smartphones to social media platforms, have transformed communication and altered relationships, social structures, and even cognitive processes.

Hot and Cool Media

McLuhan introduced the distinction between "hot" and "cool" media as a way to categorize media types based on their sensory engagement and the level of audience involvement they require. Hot media, such as print or film, provide high-definition information, meaning they contain a lot of detail and require little participation from the audience. Reading a book or watching a movie requires us to be passive recipients, as the medium provides a complete and detailed experience. Cool media, such as television or radio, on the other hand, provide lower-definition information and demand more active engagement. A television show, for example, often encourages viewers to fill in gaps or interpret visual cues, creating a participatory experience.

This concept of hot and cool media is valuable for understanding how different media formats engage audiences. By examining whether a medium is hot or cool, we gain insight into the cognitive demands it places on users and how it influences societal interaction. For example, social media platforms, which are highly interactive and require constant user engagement, might be classified as cool media in McLuhan's framework. Understanding these distinctions can help us analyse how digital media create different social and cognitive experiences compared to traditional forms.

Global Village

McLuhan's notion of the "global village" captures his belief that electronic media would fundamentally alter human connections by breaking down geographic and cultural boundaries. He predicted that technologies like radio and television would connect people across vast distances, fostering a sense of global interconnectedness. In a global village, people would become more aware of and engaged with the lives of others, regardless of physical location. This interconnectedness, McLuhan argued, would lead to a collective consciousness, where the entire world becomes like a small, interconnected community.

This idea anticipated the impact of the internet and social media, which have indeed created a global village where events in one part of the world can have immediate repercussions elsewhere. This concept remains highly relevant as we witness how digital platforms enable people to engage in global conversations, share experiences across cultures, and mobilize around issues that affect communities worldwide. However, McLuhan also recognized the potential drawbacks of this interconnectedness, such as the loss of cultural uniqueness and the spread of homogenous media content.

Media Technologies and Power: Brian Winston

Brian Winston, a prominent media historian and scholar, focused on the relationship between technology, society, and power. Winston argued that while new media technologies have the potential to disrupt existing social and economic structures, they often face resistance from powerful forces that seek to control or suppress their radical potential. His key idea, known as the "Law of the Suppression of Radical Potential," provides a framework for understanding how media technologies evolve and how their development is shaped by broader social and economic contexts.

The Law of the Suppression of Radical Potential

Winston's "Law of the Suppression of Radical Potential" suggests that media technologies initially emerge with the potential to bring about significant social change. However, this potential is frequently suppressed by existing power structures that fear losing control or profit. Governments, corporations, and other influential actors often co-opt new technologies, either by regulating them, limiting their functionality, or redirecting their development in ways that align with their interests. This suppression ensures that the new technology does not disrupt the status quo too drastically or undermine the existing power structures.

For instance, Winston pointed out that when radio was first invented, it was seen as a tool that could democratize information by allowing anyone to broadcast their ideas. However, governments quickly established regulations to control radio frequencies and licenses, ensuring that radio became a centralized, regulated industry rather than an open, public platform. In this way, the radical potential of radio was suppressed to prevent it from threatening established media and governmental control.

Factors that Shape Technological Development

Winston identified several factors that influence the development and adoption of new media technologies, including patent law, market competition, and government regulation. Patent law can be a tool for controlling innovation by granting exclusive rights to certain companies, which limits how widely a new technology can be used or modified. Market competition also plays a role, as large corporations often have the resources to acquire or control new technologies before they become widely available to the public. Additionally, government regulations can dictate how a technology is used, determining whether it serves the interests of the public or reinforces existing power structures.

An example of these factors at work can be seen in the history of the internet. Initially developed as an open network by academic and military institutions, the internet was later commercialized and dominated by large corporations. Today, tech giants like Google, Facebook, and Amazon control much of the online landscape, shaping how information is accessed and how data is collected and used. Government regulation of the internet has also increased in many countries, with some governments using it as a tool for surveillance and censorship. Thus, while the internet was initially seen as a democratizing force, its radical potential has been suppressed by corporate interests and state control.

Suppression as a Response to Social Disruption

Winston also argued that the suppression of radical potential is a response to the disruptive effects that new technologies often have on society. When a new technology emerges, it can challenge existing industries, change social norms, and create new forms of interaction. These disruptions can be threatening to established institutions, which may respond by attempting to control or limit the technology. By doing so, they protect their interests and ensure that the technology aligns with the existing social and economic order.

An example of this can be seen in the development of social media platforms. Initially celebrated as tools for free expression and grassroots activism, social media have faced increasing control through corporate algorithms, data tracking, and, in some cases, government censorship. While social media had the potential to decentralize communication and empower individuals, their radical potential has been co-opted by advertising models and data-driven algorithms that prioritize profit over public interest.

4. Postmodernism and the Media

- **Simulacra and Simulation**: Imagine watching a reality TV show. The people seem real, the situations dramatic, and the emotions raw. But how much of it is actually "real"? Baudrillard argued that in our media-saturated world, the lines between reality and representation have blurred. We are surrounded by "simulacra" - copies without originals - and "simulation" - imitations of processes or systems that may have no basis in reality. Reality TV is a perfect example. It's presented as real life, but it's carefully constructed, edited, and even scripted to create compelling narratives. The media constantly create and perpetuate these simulated realities, making it difficult to distinguish between what's authentic and what's manufactured. This constant exposure to simulacra can lead to a sense of detachment from the real world, where experiences are mediated through the lens of media representations.

- **Hyperreality**: Think about how a movie can make you feel – the excitement of a car chase, the heartbreak of a lost love, the thrill of a superhero's victory. These emotions can feel more intense and real than those experienced in everyday life. This is what Baudrillard called "hyperreality," a state where the simulated becomes more real than real. The media bombard us with vivid images, compelling narratives, and heightened emotions, creating a hyperreal world that can be more alluring and engaging than our own lived experiences. This constant immersion in hyperreality can distort our perceptions, making us crave the heightened sensations and idealized representations found in media, while potentially diminishing the value of ordinary, unmediated experiences.

- **Fragmentation and Deconstruction**: Flip through TV channels, scroll through social media, or browse online news sites. You're bombarded with a dizzying array of information, perspectives, and narratives. This is the fragmented nature of postmodern media. There's no single, unifying narrative, but rather a multitude of voices and viewpoints vying for attention. This fragmentation can be disorienting, making it difficult to construct a coherent worldview. But it can also be liberating, offering individuals the freedom to pick and choose the information and perspectives that resonate with them, creating their own personalized narratives and identities.

- **The Death of the Author**: When you read a news article or watch a movie, do you assume the author's intended meaning is the only valid interpretation? Barthes argued against this idea. He believed that the meaning of a text is not solely determined by its creator, but is also shaped by the reader or viewer. In a postmodern media landscape, audiences are active interpreters of media messages. They bring their own experiences, cultural backgrounds, and biases to the table, constructing their own meanings from the vast array of available content. This challenges the traditional notion of authorship and empowers audiences to engage critically with media, questioning dominant narratives and creating their own interpretations.

Semiotic Approach

- **Signifier and Signified**: Think of a traffic light. The red light (the signifier) is a visual cue that communicates the concept of "stop" (the signified). This is the basic principle of semiotics – the study of how signs and symbols create meaning. In media studies, semiotics helps us understand how media texts use signs to communicate complex messages. A photograph, a sound effect, a word, or a gesture can all function as signifiers, conveying specific meanings to the audience. By analysing the relationship between signifiers and signifieds, we can decode the underlying messages embedded in media texts.

- **Denotation and Connotation**: Consider the image of a lion. Its denotation is simply "a large carnivorous feline." However, the lion also carries connotations of strength, power, and royalty. These connotations are culturally and historically constructed, adding layers of meaning to the image. Semiotics helps us understand how media texts use connotations to evoke specific emotions and associations. A news report might use images of a soaring eagle to connote freedom and patriotism, while a horror film might use dark, shadowy lighting to connote fear and suspense. By analysing denotations and connotations, we can uncover the subtle ways in which media texts shape our perceptions and emotions.

- **Codes and Conventions**: Think about the typical elements of a Western movie – cowboys, saloons, gunfights, and dusty landscapes. These are codes and conventions that have become associated with the genre. Media texts rely on these shared codes to communicate meaning efficiently. Audiences have learned to interpret these codes, allowing them to quickly understand the genre, setting, and characters of a story. Semiotics helps us identify and analyse these codes, revealing how media texts draw on shared cultural knowledge to create meaning. By understanding these codes, we can gain a deeper appreciation for the artistry of media production and the complex ways in which meaning is constructed.

Semiotic Approach: Unraveling the Language of Media

Semiotics, the study of signs and symbols, provides a powerful lens for dissecting media messages and understanding how meaning is created and communicated. It equips us with the tools to decode the intricate language of media, uncovering hidden meanings and revealing the subtle ways in which media texts shape our perceptions, values, and beliefs.

The Building Blocks of Meaning: Signifier and Signified

At the heart of semiotics lies the concept of the sign, which is anything that stands for something else. Ferdinand de Saussure, a Swiss linguist and the father of modern semiotics, broke down the sign into two components: the signifier and the signified.

- **The Signifier:** This is the physical form of the sign – the word, image, sound, or gesture that we perceive through our senses. For example, the image of a red rose is a signifier.

- **The Signified:** This is the concept or meaning that the signifier represents. In our example, the signified might be love, passion, or romance.

The relationship between the signifier and the signified is arbitrary, meaning there is no natural or inherent connection between them. It is through cultural conventions and shared understanding that we learn to associate certain signifiers with specific meanings.

Layers of Meaning: Denotation and Connotation

Roland Barthes, a French literary theorist, expanded on Saussure's ideas by introducing the concepts of denotation and connotation.

- **Denotation:** This refers to the literal or dictionary meaning of a sign. For example, the denotation of the word "snake" is a long, legless reptile.

- **Connotation:** This refers to the associated meanings or implications of a sign, often shaped by cultural and personal experiences. The connotation of "snake" might be danger, deception, or evil, depending on the cultural context and individual interpretations.

Media texts often rely on connotations to evoke specific emotions and associations. A news report might use images of a dove to connote peace and hope, while an advertisement might use images of a fast car to connote speed, excitement, and success. By analysing denotations and connotations, we can uncover the subtle ways in which media texts influence our perceptions and emotions.

The Grammar of Media: Codes and Conventions

Just as language has grammar rules, media texts employ codes and conventions to structure their messages and communicate meaning effectively. These codes can be visual, auditory, or linguistic.

- **Visual Codes:** These include elements like color, composition, lighting, camera angles, and editing techniques. For example, a horror film might use dark lighting and distorted camera angles to create a sense of unease and suspense.

- **Auditory Codes:** These involve the use of sound effects, music, and dialogue. A romantic comedy might use upbeat music and witty dialogue to create a lighthearted and humorous tone.

- **Linguistic Codes:** These encompass the use of language, including word choice, sentence structure, and narrative style. A news report might use formal language and objective tone to convey authority and credibility.

By understanding these codes and conventions, we can decipher the underlying messages embedded in media texts. We can recognize how certain genres, like Westerns or romantic comedies, use specific codes to evoke familiar emotions and expectations. We can also identify how media producers use codes to manipulate our perceptions and reinforce certain ideologies.

Decoding the Media Landscape

Semiotic analysis provides a framework for critically examining media texts and understanding how they create meaning. Here are some key approaches to analysing media through a semiotic lens:

- **Identifying Signs and Symbols:** Start by identifying the key signs and symbols used in the media text. What are the dominant images, sounds, and words? What do they represent?
- **Analysing Denotations and Connotations:** Consider both the denotative and connotative meanings of the signs. What are the literal meanings? What are the associated meanings and cultural implications?
- **Deciphering Codes and Conventions:** Identify the codes and conventions used in the text. How do they contribute to the overall message? How do they shape our understanding of the genre, characters, and narrative?
- **Considering Context:** Analyse the media text in its broader social and cultural context. How does the text reflect or challenge dominant ideologies and values? How does it relate to other media texts and cultural trends?
- **Interpreting Meaning:** Remember that meaning is not fixed or inherent in the text itself. It is constructed through the interaction between the text and the audience. Consider how different audiences might interpret the same text based on their own cultural backgrounds, personal experiences, and values.

The Power of Semiotics

Semiotics empowers us to become critical consumers of media, recognizing the subtle ways in which media texts shape our perceptions and beliefs. By understanding the language of media, we can engage with media more consciously and thoughtfully, questioning dominant narratives and constructing our own interpretations.

In a world saturated with media messages, semiotics provides a crucial toolkit for navigating the complex landscape of signs and symbols. It allows us to unravel the hidden meanings embedded in media texts, revealing the power dynamics, cultural assumptions, and ideological messages that shape our understanding of the world.

Postmodernism and the Media: Navigating a World of Simulacra

Postmodernism, a complex and multifaceted movement that emerged in the late 20th century, challenges many of the assumptions of modernism, particularly the notion of objective truth and a stable, unified reality. In the realm of media studies, postmodernism offers a critical lens for analysing the fragmented, hyperreal, and often contradictory nature of contemporary media culture.

Key Concepts:

- **Simulacra and Simulation:** Jean Baudrillard, a prominent French sociologist and philosopher, argued that in our media-saturated world, the distinction between reality and representation has collapsed. We are surrounded by "simulacra" – copies without originals – and "simulation" – the imitation of a process or system that may have no basis in reality.

Think of reality TV shows, where "real people" are placed in contrived situations, their lives edited and manipulated to create compelling narratives. Or consider the carefully curated images on social media, where individuals present idealized versions of themselves, blurring the lines between their online persona and their offline reality. These are examples of simulacra and simulation, where the representation becomes more real than the real, shaping our perceptions and desires. Baudrillard identified four phases of the image:

* **1st order:** The image is a reflection of a basic reality.
* **2nd order:** The image masks and perverts a basic reality.
* **3rd order:** The image masks the *absence* of a basic reality.
* **4th order:** The image bears no relation to any reality whatsoever - it is its own pure simulacrum.

He argued that we have entered the fourth order, where images and simulations have become detached from any underlying reality, creating a hyperreal world that is more vivid and engaging than actual experiences.

- **Hyperreality:** This concept describes a state where the simulated becomes more real than the real, where media representations are more alluring and engaging than actual experiences. We are constantly bombarded with images and narratives that create a hyperreal world, shaping our perceptions and desires.

Consider the immersive experience of video games, where players can inhabit virtual worlds that are often more exciting and fulfilling than their everyday lives. Or think of the way advertising uses idealized images and aspirational narratives to create a sense of longing and dissatisfaction with our current reality. This constant immersion in hyperreality can distort our perceptions, making us crave the heightened sensations and idealized representations found in media, while potentially diminishing the value of ordinary, unmediated experiences.

- **Fragmentation and Deconstruction:** Postmodernism emphasizes the fragmented and decentralized nature of contemporary culture. The media reflect this fragmentation by offering a vast array of choices and perspectives, making it difficult to construct a coherent worldview.

With the proliferation of cable channels, streaming services, and online content, we are constantly exposed to a multitude of voices and viewpoints, often contradictory and competing. This fragmentation can be disorienting, but it can also be liberating, allowing individuals to construct their own meanings and identities from the multitude of available options.

- **The Death of the Author:** Roland Barthes, a French literary theorist, challenged the notion that the meaning of a text is determined solely by its author. He argued that the reader plays an active role in interpreting and constructing meaning.

In a postmodern media landscape, audiences are empowered to create their own interpretations of media messages, drawing on their own experiences and cultural contexts. This challenges the traditional notion of authorship and encourages audiences to engage critically with media, questioning dominant narratives and creating their own meanings.

Analysing Media through a Postmodern Lens

Postmodernism provides a framework for critically analysing media texts and understanding how they shape our perceptions, values, and social interactions. Here are some key approaches:

- **Deconstructing Media Texts:** Postmodern analysis involves dissecting media texts to reveal their underlying assumptions, contradictions, and hidden meanings. This might involve examining how different social groups are represented, how power relations are encoded, and how the text constructs a particular version of reality.
- **Analysing Media Spectacles:** Postmodernism is interested in how the media create spectacular events and images that capture our attention and shape our perceptions. This might involve analysing how media events like celebrity scandals, political campaigns, and sporting events are constructed and consumed, and how they contribute to the hyperreal.
- **Exploring the Relationship between Media and Identity:** In a postmodern world, identity is seen as fluid and fragmented, shaped by a multitude of influences, including the media. Postmodern analysis might explore how individuals construct their identities through their engagement with media culture, drawing on the diverse and often contradictory representations available.

The Postmodern Challenge

Postmodernism challenges us to question the reality presented to us by the media, to recognize the power of simulacra and simulation, and to engage critically with the fragmented and hyperreal nature of contemporary media culture. It encourages us to become active interpreters of media messages, constructing our own meanings and challenging dominant narratives. In a world where the lines between reality and representation are increasingly blurred, postmodernism offers a critical lens for navigating the complex and ever-evolving media landscape.

Analysing Media Through a Postmodern Lens: Deconstructing the Hyperreal

Postmodernism provides a powerful toolkit for dissecting media messages and understanding how they operate in our increasingly complex and media-saturated world. Here's how we can apply a postmodern lens to analyse media texts:

Deconstructing Media Texts:

This approach involves peeling back the layers of a media text to reveal its underlying assumptions, contradictions, and hidden meanings. It's like taking apart a machine to understand how it works, but instead of gears and wires, we're looking at signs, codes, and narratives.

- **Identifying the Constructed Nature of Reality:** Postmodernism challenges the notion of a singular, objective reality. Instead, it emphasizes that reality is constructed through language, discourse, and representation. When analysing a media text, ask yourself: How does this text construct a particular version of reality? What are the underlying assumptions and biases that shape this representation?
- **Unmasking Power Relations:** Media texts often reinforce or challenge existing power structures. Analyse how different social groups are represented. Who has a voice? Who is silenced or marginalized? How are gender, race, class, and other social categories portrayed? Look for stereotypes, biases, and power imbalances embedded in the text.
- **Exposing Contradictions and Ambiguities:** Postmodernism embraces contradictions and ambiguities, recognizing that meaning is not always fixed or straightforward. Look for inconsistencies, paradoxes, and multiple interpretations within the text. How does the text challenge our expectations or subvert conventional narratives?
- **Analysing Language and Discourse:** Language is not neutral; it shapes our understanding of the world. Pay attention to the language used in the media text. What are the dominant metaphors, narratives, and discourses? How do they frame the issue or event being depicted? How do they shape our understanding and emotions?
-

Analysing Media Spectacles:

In a postmodern world, media spectacles – those grand, attention-grabbing events and images – play a crucial role in shaping our perceptions and desires. These spectacles can be anything from celebrity scandals and political campaigns to sporting events and disaster coverage.

- **Deconstructing the Spectacle:** Analyse how the spectacle is constructed. What are the key elements that make it captivating? How is it staged, edited, and presented to maximize its impact? What emotions does it evoke?
- **Unmasking the Underlying Messages:** Media spectacles often carry hidden messages and ideologies. What are the underlying values and beliefs being promoted? How does the spectacle reinforce or challenge dominant narratives?
- **Understanding the Role of the Audience:** Audiences are not passive consumers of spectacles; they actively participate in their construction and interpretation. How does the media encourage audience engagement and participation? How do audiences interpret and respond to the spectacle?
- **Critiquing the Culture of Spectacle:** Postmodernism critiques the way media spectacles can distract us from more critical issues and reinforce consumerism and superficiality. How does the spectacle contribute to the hyperreal? How does it shape our desires and values?

Exploring the Relationship between Media and Identity:

In a postmodern world, identity is fluid, fragmented, and constantly evolving. The media play a significant role in shaping how we understand ourselves and our place in the world.

- **Analysing Representations of Identity:** Examine how different identities – gender, race, sexuality, class, etc. – are represented in the media. Look for stereotypes, biases, and alternative representations. How do these representations shape our understanding of ourselves and others?
- **Understanding the Construction of Identity:** Postmodernism emphasizes that identity is not fixed or inherent; it is constructed through social interactions and cultural representations. How do media texts contribute to the construction of identity? How do individuals use media to express and explore their identities?
- **Navigating the Fragmentation of Identity:** In a media-saturated world, we are exposed to a multitude of identities and lifestyles. How do individuals navigate this fragmented landscape? How do they construct coherent identities in the face of competing narratives and representations?
- **Critiquing the Commodification of Identity:** Postmodernism critiques the way media can commodify and commercialize identity, turning it into a product to be consumed. How do media

texts promote certain lifestyles and identities as desirable? How do they encourage individuals to consume products and experiences to construct their identities?

By applying these analytical tools, we can gain a deeper understanding of how media operates in a postmodern world. We can deconstruct media texts, analyse spectacles, and explore the complex relationship between media and identity. This allows us to engage with media more critically, challenge dominant narratives, and construct our own meanings in a world of simulacra and hyperreality.

Psychoanalytic Approach to Media: Delving into the Depths of Desire

The psychoanalytic approach to media draws upon the theories of Sigmund Freud and his successors to explore the unconscious desires, anxieties, and fantasies that shape our engagement with media texts. It delves beneath the surface of media content to uncover the hidden psychological processes at play, revealing how media can tap into our deepest fears and desires.

Key Concepts:

- **The Unconscious:** Freud's groundbreaking concept of the unconscious revolutionized our understanding of the human psyche. He argued that our thoughts, feelings, and behaviours are largely driven by unconscious forces, hidden desires, and repressed memories. The psychoanalytic approach to media examines how media texts can tap into these unconscious processes, triggering emotions and associations that we may not be fully aware of.
- **The Oedipus Complex:** This cornerstone of Freudian theory describes a child's unconscious desire for their opposite-sex parent and rivalry with their same-sex parent. In media studies, the Oedipus complex can be used to analyse how narratives and characters often play out these primal desires and conflicts. For example, many films and TV shows feature love triangles and power struggles that resonate with Oedipal themes.
- **Scopophilia and Voyeurism:** Scopophilia refers to the pleasure of looking, while voyeurism refers to the pleasure of looking at someone without their knowledge. The psychoanalytic approach examines how media can gratify these desires, allowing us to gaze upon others and delve into their private lives. Reality TV,

celebrity gossip, and even fictional narratives can offer a sense of voyeuristic pleasure, fulfilling our curiosity about the lives of others.

- **Identification and Projection:** We often identify with characters in media texts, projecting our own desires and anxieties onto them. This identification can be a source of both pleasure and discomfort, as we experience the characters' triumphs and struggles as our own. Psychoanalytic analysis can explore how media texts encourage identification and how this process can shape our own sense of self.

Laura Mulvey and the Male Gaze:

One of the most influential figures in the psychoanalytic approach to media is Laura Mulvey, a British feminist film theorist. Her groundbreaking essay, "Visual Pleasure and Narrative Cinema" (1975), introduced the concept of the "male gaze."

- **The Male Gaze:** Mulvey argued that mainstream cinema is structured around a "male gaze" that objectifies and sexualizes female characters. The camera often lingers on women's bodies, framing them as objects of visual pleasure for the male spectator. This objectification, Mulvey argued, reinforces patriarchal power structures and contributes to the subordination of women in society.
- **Voyeurism and Fetishism:** Mulvey also explored how the male gaze is linked to voyeuristic and fetishist desires. The camera allows the spectator to gaze upon women without their knowledge, fulfilling a sense of voyeuristic pleasure. Furthermore, the male gaze often fragments women's bodies, focusing on specific body parts as objects of fetishist desire. This fragmentation denies women their subjectivity and reduces them to objects of male pleasure.

Analysing Media through a Psychoanalytic Lens:

The psychoanalytic approach offers a rich framework for analysing media texts and understanding how they tap into our deepest desires and anxieties. Here are some key approaches:

- **Analysing Characters and Narratives:** Explore the psychological motivations of characters. What are their unconscious desires and anxieties? How do their actions and relationships reflect psychoanalytic concepts like the Oedipus complex or defense mechanisms?

- **Examining Visual and Auditory Cues:** Pay attention to the visual and auditory elements of the media text. How do camera angles, lighting, music, and sound effects contribute to the emotional impact of the text? How do they trigger unconscious associations and emotions?
- **Considering Audience Response:** Analyse how the media text is likely to be received by different audiences. How might it tap into their unconscious desires and anxieties? How might it reinforce or challenge their existing beliefs and values?
- **Critiquing Media's Influence:** The psychoanalytic approach can be used to critique the way media can manipulate our desires and anxieties, promoting consumerism, reinforcing stereotypes, or perpetuating harmful ideologies.

Beyond Mulvey: Expanding the Psychoanalytic Approach:

While Mulvey's work has been highly influential, the psychoanalytic approach to media has continued to evolve, incorporating new perspectives and addressing a wider range of media texts.

- **Queer Theory and Psychoanalysis:** Queer theorists have used psychoanalysis to analyse representations of sexuality and gender in media, challenging heteronormative assumptions and exploring the complexities of desire.
- **Race and Psychoanalysis:** Scholars have used psychoanalysis to examine the psychological impact of racial stereotypes and discrimination in media.
- **New Media and Psychoanalysis:** The rise of new media, such as social media and video games, has opened up new avenues for psychoanalytic inquiry, exploring how these technologies shape our identities, relationships, and sense of self.

The Enduring Power of Psychoanalysis:

The psychoanalytic approach to media remains a powerful tool for understanding the complex interplay between media, the unconscious, and the human psyche. By delving into the depths of desire, it can reveal the hidden meanings and motivations that shape our engagement with media texts, offering insights into the profound ways in which media can influence our thoughts, feelings, and behaviours.

Expanding the Psychoanalytic Lens: New Frontiers in Media Studies

While the classic concepts of psychoanalysis remain relevant, the field of media studies has evolved, incorporating new perspectives and addressing the complexities of our ever-changing media landscape. Here are some key areas where the psychoanalytic approach continues to offer valuable insights:

Queer Theory and Psychoanalysis:

Queer theory challenges traditional notions of sexuality and gender, questioning the binary categories and exploring the fluidity of desire. Psychoanalysis provides a useful framework for understanding the complexities of queer representation in media.

- **Challenging Heteronormativity:** Queer theorists use psychoanalysis to deconstruct heteronormative assumptions in media texts, exposing how these assumptions can reinforce social norms and marginalize non-heterosexual identities.
- **Exploring Queer Desire:** Psychoanalysis can help illuminate the diverse forms of desire and identification that exist beyond the heterosexual paradigm. By analysing queer characters and narratives, we can gain a deeper understanding of the fluidity and complexities of human sexuality.
- **Analysing the Psychoanalytic Construction of Gender:** Queer theory draws on psychoanalysis to examine how gender is constructed and performed in media. It explores how media texts can both reinforce and subvert traditional gender roles and expectations.

Race and Psychoanalysis:

The psychoanalytic approach can be used to examine the psychological impact of racial stereotypes and discrimination in media.
- **Unconscious Bias and Stereotypes:** Psychoanalysis can help uncover the unconscious biases and stereotypes that shape media representations of race. It can reveal how these representations can perpetuate harmful prejudices and reinforce social inequalities.
- **Trauma and Representation:** Psychoanalysis can provide insights into the psychological effects of trauma, particularly in relation to representations of historical events and social

injustices. It can help us understand how media can both contribute to and help heal from collective trauma.

- **Identity Formation and Race:** Psychoanalysis can explore how racial identity is formed and negotiated in a media-saturated world. It can examine how media representations can influence individuals' sense of self and their relationships with others.

New Media and Psychoanalysis:

The rise of new media, such as social media, video games, and virtual reality, has opened up new avenues for psychoanalytic inquiry.

- **Identity and the Digital Self:** Psychoanalysis can help us understand how individuals construct and perform their identities in online spaces. It can explore the psychological motivations behind social media use and the impact of digital technologies on our sense of self.
- **Virtual Worlds and Fantasy:** Psychoanalysis can be used to analyse the immersive experiences offered by video games and virtual reality. It can explore how these technologies tap into our fantasies and desires, providing spaces for exploration and escape.
- **Social Media and Relationships:** Psychoanalysis can help us understand the dynamics of online relationships and the psychological impact of social media on our social interactions and emotional well-being.

4. Beyond the Individual: Psychoanalysis and the Social

While psychoanalysis often focuses on the individual psyche, it can also be applied to understand broader social and cultural phenomena.

- **Collective Unconscious:** Carl Jung, a Swiss psychoanalyst, introduced the concept of the "collective unconscious," a shared reservoir of archetypes and symbols that are common to all humanity. This concept can be used to analyse how media texts tap into universal themes and myths that resonate across cultures.
- **Ideology and the Unconscious:** Psychoanalysis can help uncover the unconscious processes that contribute to the acceptance and perpetuation of ideologies. It can reveal how media texts can manipulate our desires and anxieties to promote certain beliefs and values.

- **Media and the Social Imaginary:** The psychoanalytic approach can be used to analyse how media contribute to the construction of the "social imaginary," the shared beliefs and values that shape our understanding of society and our place within it.

The Future of Psychoanalytic Media Studies

The psychoanalytic approach to media continues to evolve, offering new insights into the complex relationship between media, the unconscious, and the human psyche. As our media landscape continues to transform, psychoanalysis will remain a valuable tool for understanding the profound ways in which media shape our perceptions, emotions, and behaviours. By delving into the depths of desire, it can illuminate the hidden meanings and motivations that drive our engagement with media, offering a critical perspective on the power of media in our lives.

The Feminist Perspective: Revealing Gender Dynamics in Media and Communication Introduction

In the domain of media and communication, where narratives are constructed and societal norms are both reflected and influenced, the feminist perspective serves as a vital lens, revealing the complex ways in which gender dynamics infiltrate our media environment. This viewpoint contests the conventional, frequently patriarchal, frameworks that have prevailed in media production and representation, providing a sophisticated comprehension of the intersection of gender with other social categories, including race, class, and sexuality. Feminist media studies enhance a more equal and inclusive media landscape by deconstructing media messages, analysing power dynamics, and campaigning for improved representation.

Historical Context: The Advent of Feminist Media Studies

Feminist media studies originated in the late 20th century, concurrent with wider feminist movements that contested conventional gender roles and promoted women's rights. Early feminist scholars scrutinised the depiction of women in media, emphasising the ubiquity of stereotypes, objectification, and under-representation. They contended that media frequently reinforced patriarchal standards, constraining women's societal responsibilities and perpetuating gender disparities.

Fundamental Principles in Feminist Media Studies

Gender Representation: Feminist scholars scrutinise the depiction of women and men in media, investigating the prevalence of stereotypes, the variety of roles they assume, and the power dynamics embedded in these portrayals. They criticise the objectification and sexualisation of women in media, contending that such representations facilitate the normalisation of gender-based violence and discrimination.

Laura Mulvey's seminal concept of the "male gaze" elucidates how mainstream media, especially film, is frequently constructed from a male viewpoint that objectifies and sexualises female characters. This gaze undermines women's autonomy and perpetuates patriarchal power dynamics.

Gendered Media Production: Feminist researchers investigate the gendered dynamics of media production, emphasising the under-representation of women in influential and decision-making roles. This deficiency in variety fosters the continuation of biassed narratives and constricted viewpoints in media output.

Intersectionality: Feminist media studies acknowledge that gender intersects with many social categories, including race, class, and sexuality, resulting in distinct experiences and challenges for individuals. This intersectional approach examines media representations of individuals at these intersections, emphasising the intricacies of identity and power interactions.

The Influence of Media on Gender and Society

Feminist researchers contend that media significantly influences gender and society, moulding our beliefs, attitudes, and behaviours. Media portrayals can shape our comprehension of gender norms, expectations, and potentialities. They may also facilitate the normalisation of gender-based violence and discrimination.

The media's depiction of idealised beauty standards, frequently unrealistic for the majority of women, can adversely affect body image and self-esteem. This may result in eating problems, body dysmorphia, and additional mental health complications.

Gender-Based Violence: The normalisation of violence against women in media, exemplified by depictions of sexual assault, domestic violence, and harassment, may facilitate the continuation of these detrimental behaviours within society.

Gender Stereotypes: Media frequently perpetuates gender stereotypes, constraining the spectrum of roles and opportunities for both women and men. This may limit individuals' options and ambitions, hence perpetuating gender disparities.

Feminist Praxis

Feminist media studies critique current media portrayals and systems while simultaneously advocating for reform. Feminist praxis entails actively confronting gender disparities in media, advocating for equitable representation, and constructing alternative narratives that empower women while contesting patriarchal norms.

Feminist media makers and campaigners confront prejudices by depicting women in varied roles, highlighting their strengths, complexities, and autonomy. They also promote more complex representations of males, contesting conventional concepts of masculinity.

Advocating for Diversity: Feminist media praxis underscores the significance of diversity in media representation and creation. This entails promoting the inclusion of women, people of colour, LGBTQ+ individuals, and other marginalised groups in positions of authority and decision-making.

Feminist media makers generate alternative narratives that contest prevailing patriarchal discourses. They narrate tales from women's viewpoints, emphasise their experiences, and commemorate their accomplishments.

The Digital Era: Emerging Challenges and Prospects

The emergence of digital media has introduced both novel obstacles and opportunities for feminist media studies. The internet and social media have facilitated outlets for various perspectives and feminist activity, allowing women to connect, share their narratives, and contest patriarchal conventions. Conversely, online environments have emerged as fertile grounds for cyberbullying, harassment, and hate speech, disproportionately affecting women and marginalised communities.

Final Assessment

The feminist perspective on media and communication provides a critical framework for analysing the widespread gender dynamics that influence our media environment. Feminist media studies enhance a more equal and inclusive media landscape by deconstructing media messages, analysing power dynamics, and campaigning for improved representation.

In a society where media significantly influences our views, attitudes, and behaviours, the feminist perspective is crucial for contesting patriarchal norms, advancing gender equality, and fostering a media environment that represents the varied experiences and voices of all individuals.

CHAPTER III

MEDIA AND SOCIAL STRUCTURE

Mass media significantly influences the formation of social structures and relationships within society. Mass media, encompassing newspapers, television, and social media platforms, serves not only as a conduit for entertainment and information but also as a formidable force that shapes public opinion, constructs identities, and sustains social norms. This section investigates the intricate relationship between mass media and social structure, analysing how media influences, mirrors, and sustains societal dynamics, encompassing class, race, gender, and power.

The Function of Mass Media in Society

Mass media fulfils several critical roles in society, including informing, educating, and entertaining the populace. It serves as a medium for communication, enabling individuals to obtain a wide range of information and viewpoints. Nonetheless, the importance of mass media transcends simple information distribution; it also serves a vital function in socialising individuals, influencing cultural norms, and forming collective identities.

Mass media influences public discourse by framing issues and determining what is deemed newsworthy. The depiction of social movements, political events, and cultural phenomena shapes public perception of these issues. The media's framing can establish dominant narratives that marginalise alternative perspectives and voices. By emphasising specific narratives while neglecting others, mass media can influence public perceptions and perpetuate established power dynamics.

Media as a Reflection of Societal Structure

The relationship between mass media and social structure is bidirectional; media not only mirrors societal values and norms but also influences their formation. Media content often mirrors the existing social order, presenting narratives and representations that align with the dominant ideology. For example, mainstream media frequently portrays gender roles, racial stereotypes, and class distinctions in ways that reinforce existing hierarchies. These representations can significantly influence individuals' perceptions of their societal roles and their interactions with others.

101

Sociologists have extensively studied the portrayal of marginalised groups in mass media. Research indicates that media frequently reinforces stereotypes and generates unrealistic representations of specific demographics, including women, people of colour, and LGBTQ+ individuals. Such representations can shape public perceptions, thereby reinforcing societal biases and discrimination. The depiction of racial minorities in crime-related news can exacerbate societal fears and perpetuate stereotypes of criminality linked to those groups.

Furthermore, media ownership and control significantly influence the content accessible to audiences. The consolidation of media ownership among a limited number of corporations can restrict the variety of perspectives and narratives available to the public. This monopolization of media resources often prioritizes profit over public interest, resulting in a homogenized media landscape that reflects the values and interests of the ruling class.

The Influence of Media on Social Relationships

Mass media impacts social relationships by determining the manner in which individuals engage and interact with each other. The emergence of digital media, especially social media platforms, has revolutionised communication and social interaction. Traditional media typically operated as a unidirectional communication channel, whereas social media facilitates more interactive and participatory engagement. Users can now create, share, and comment on content, fostering a sense of community and collective identity.

However, the impact of social media on social relationships is complex. While it can facilitate connections and support networks, it can also lead to fragmentation and isolation. The curated nature of social media feeds often results in echo chambers, where individuals are exposed to information that aligns with their existing beliefs and values. This phenomenon can reinforce existing biases and polarize public opinion, hindering constructive dialogue and understanding between different groups.

Additionally, the rise of online interactions raises questions about authenticity and the quality of social relationships. The mediated nature of communication can lead to superficial connections, where individuals prioritize quantity over quality in their social networks. The emphasis on likes, shares, and followers can create pressure to present an idealized version of oneself, leading to issues of self-esteem and identity among users.

Media and Audience

The interplay between media and audience is a fundamental concept in media sociology. This relationship is not simply one of passive consumption; rather, it entails a complex interaction of influence, interpretation, and negotiation. Audiences actively interact with media texts, incorporating their personal experiences, beliefs, and cultural backgrounds into the process of interpretation. This section analyses the dynamics of media-audience interactions, focussing on how audiences respond to, interpret, and occasionally resist media messages.

Audience as Engaged Participants

Historically, media scholars regarded audiences as passive recipients of content, vulnerable to the persuasive influence of mass media. Contemporary research highlights the active role audiences assume in interpreting and negotiating media messages. Audiences are heterogeneous, consisting of diverse groups with differing cultural backgrounds, experiences, and values. This diversity affects individuals' reactions to media content and the interpretations they extract from it.

Theories of audience reception, including Stuart Hall's encoding/decoding model, underscore the intricacy of this relationship. Hall contended that media texts are imbued with particular meanings by producers, yet audiences interpret these messages variably according to their unique contexts. The decoding process yields three principal interpretations: dominant (accepting the intended meaning), negotiated (partially accepting the intended meaning while contesting certain elements), and oppositional (entirely rejecting the intended meaning). This model demonstrates that audience engagement is an active process in which individuals negotiate their comprehension of media texts.

Determinants Affecting Audience Reception

Numerous factors affect audience engagement with media content, such as cultural background, personal experiences, and social context. An individual's cultural identity can influence their interpretation of representations of race, gender, or sexuality in media. Media content that aligns with cultural experiences may be accepted, whereas content that reinforces stereotypes or misrepresents identity may be dismissed or condemned.

Furthermore, the social context of media consumption significantly influences audience reception. Peer influence, family dynamics, and community norms can affect individual engagement with media. A person's interpretation of a controversial news story may vary based on whether they are conversing with like-minded friends or interacting with individuals from varied backgrounds.

The emergence of digital media has significantly altered audience engagement. Digital platforms facilitate instantaneous interactions and dialogues concerning media content, permitting audiences to articulate their viewpoints, disseminate their interpretations, and participate in collaborative meaning construction. Social media platforms have emerged as venues for audiences to critique and contest media representations, fostering opportunities for activism and social transformation.

Impact of Media on Public Perception

The media exerts considerable influence on public perception and opinion. The portrayal of issues in media narratives can influence audience comprehension and reactions to societal challenges. The depiction of public health matters, such as the COVID-19 pandemic, in news media can influence individual risk perception and compliance with health directives. Media framing can influence public perceptions of marginalised groups, thereby shaping societal norms and values.

Studies indicate that frequent exposure to particular media narratives can result in the normalisation of certain beliefs and behaviours. Depictions of violence in film and television may foster desensitisation and the acceptance of aggressive behaviour within society. This normalization process can have profound implications for public policy and social attitudes, particularly regarding issues such as crime, immigration, and mental health.

Opposition and Autonomy

Audiences frequently negotiate and interpret media messages, but they can also assert agency by resisting prevailing narratives. Social movements and grassroots organisations have progressively employed media to enhance marginalised voices and contest dominant ideologies. The emergence of alternative media platforms enables audiences to produce and distribute their content, providing counter-narratives that challenge mainstream media portrayals.

Moreover, audience resistance may be expressed through boycotts, social media initiatives, and public demonstrations opposing media practices considered detrimental or deceptive. This active involvement indicates an increasing consciousness of the power dynamics inherent in media production and consumption, as audiences strive to hold media institutions accountable for their representations and narratives.

The relationship between media and audience is complex and multifaceted, characterized by active engagement, interpretation, and negotiation. Understanding this relationship is crucial for analysing how media shapes public perception, social norms, and cultural identities. By recognizing the agency of audiences in the media landscape, scholars can better understand the dynamics of power, representation, and resistance that define contemporary media practices.

Media-Media Ethics

The convergence of media and ethics constitutes a vital domain of investigation within media sociology. Given that media institutions possess considerable authority in shaping public discourse, representing varied perspectives, and influencing societal values, ethical considerations are essential. This section investigates the ethical dilemmas and responsibilities inherent in media production and consumption, analysing their implications for individuals, communities, and society as a whole.

Establishing Media Ethics

Media ethics comprises a collection of principles and standards that direct the behaviour of media professionals in their duties. These ethical frameworks seek to guarantee precision, equity, and responsibility in media practices. Essential ethical considerations encompass veracity, transparency, respect for confidentiality, and the obligation to prevent harm. Media professionals must navigate intricate ethical dilemmas, especially in a swiftly evolving media environment marked by technological progress and changing audience expectations.

A fundamental tenet of media ethics is the dedication to truth and precision. Journalists, filmmakers, and content creators bear the obligation to furnish accurate information and offer a balanced perspective on issues. Nonetheless, the imperative to captivate audiences and yield profit may occasionally result in sensationalism, misinformation, and partial reporting. The proliferation of "fake news" and disinformation campaigns has highlighted the necessity of ethical practices to uphold public trust in media institutions.

Ethical Considerations in Media Representation

Media representation constitutes a critical ethical issue, especially concerning marginalised populations. The representation of race, gender, sexuality, and class in media can significantly influence societal perceptions and personal identities. Ethical media practices necessitate awareness of the effects of representations on various communities, aiming to eliminate stereotypes and foster diversity.

The under-representation or misrepresentation of people of colour, women, and LGBTQ+ individuals in media can perpetuate detrimental narratives and reinforce societal inequities. Media producers bear the obligation to incorporate diverse voices and perspectives, guaranteeing that their content mirrors the intricacies of the human experience. Ethical media practices promote the involvement of marginalised communities in the creation process, enabling individuals to narrate their own stories and influence their representations.

Furthermore, ethical dilemmas emerge when media content pertains to sensitive topics, including trauma, violence, and mental health. Media professionals must balance the imperative of raising awareness about significant issues with the obligation to uphold the dignity and privacy of individuals impacted by these matters. Ethical principles require that media refrain from exploitative practices and emphasise informed consent when depicting vulnerable individuals.

The Function of Media Organisations

Media institutions are essential in maintaining ethical standards and practices. Professional organisations, including the Society of Professional Journalists (SPJ) and the American Psychological Association (APA), formulate ethical codes that offer directives for media practitioners. These codes function as frameworks for ethical decision-making, fostering accountability and transparency in media practices.

Moreover, media organisations should emphasise ethical training and education for their personnel. By cultivating a culture of ethical awareness and accountability, media organisations can alleviate ethical dilemmas and encourage best practices. This entails promoting candid dialogues regarding ethical dilemmas and supplying resources for employees to manage intricate circumstances.

Audience Accountability and Media Engagement

Media producers hold substantial ethical responsibilities, while audiences also play an essential role in media ethics. Media consumers must critically evaluate content and contemplate the ethical ramifications of their consumption decisions. This entails being cognisant of information sources, scrutinising representations, and promoting ethical standards in media production.

In an age of information saturation, audience media literacy is crucial for promoting ethical media consumption. Media literacy programs seek to empower individuals with the competencies to analyse, assess, and produce media content. Through the promotion of critical thinking and ethical awareness, media literacy enables audiences to hold media institutions accountable and advocate for elevated ethical standards.

MASS MEDIA IN THE INDIAN CONTEXT

Mass Media and Social Framework in India

In India, mass media functions as a vital conduit between the government, society, and individuals, significantly influencing social structures and cultural narratives. The Indian mass media landscape features a variety of platforms, including print, radio, television, and digital media, each uniquely contributing to Indian society. This section analyses the complex interplay between mass media and social structure, investigating how media shapes and mirrors social dynamics, cultural identities, and power relations in the Indian context.

Comprehending the Social Structure in India

India's social structure is characterised by its complexity, encompassing diverse castes, religions, languages, and regional identities. This diversity influences the functioning and consumption of mass media across various societal segments. Media representations frequently mirror the traditional hierarchies and power dynamics inherent in Indian society. Media not only disseminates information but also reinforces or contests prevailing social norms and values.

Media as an Instrument for Social Integration

Mass media in India serves a crucial function in promoting social integration by offering a shared platform for varied perspectives. National television channels frequently air programs that honour cultural diversity, foster national unity, and emphasise common values. During pivotal events, such as national celebrations or crises, the media serves as an instrument for galvanising public sentiment and cultivating a sense of unity among the heterogeneous populace. This is especially apparent in the manner in which media coverage of events such as Independence Day or Republic Day fosters a unified national identity.

Media Representation and Power Structures

Nonetheless, the portrayal of diverse social groups in the media may also reinforce prevailing inequalities. The representation of marginalised communities, including lower castes, tribal populations, and women, frequently mirrors societal prejudices, perpetuating stereotypes and diminishing their visibility. News narratives concerning caste violence or gender-based discrimination often neglect to amplify the perspectives of those impacted, instead presenting these issues from a viewpoint that favours dominant groups. This under-representation can intensify existing social disparities and impede social advancement.

The Function of Contemporary Media

The emergence of new media technologies has exacerbated the complexity of the relationship between mass media and social structure. The emergence of the internet and social media platforms has democratised content creation, enabling individuals from varied backgrounds to disseminate their narratives and viewpoints. This transition may disrupt conventional media narratives and confront prevailing power structures. Grassroots movements utilising social media have gained momentum in India, allowing marginalised groups to organise, advocate for their rights, and raise awareness of social injustices.

Nonetheless, this democratisation presents challenges. The digital divide persists as a critical concern, with internet access varying among diverse socio-economic groups. Rural communities, women, and individuals from lower castes frequently encounter obstacles to digital engagement, constraining their capacity to participate in and shape media narratives. The proliferation of misinformation and hate speech on social media platforms raises concerns regarding the quality of discourse and its effects on social cohesion.

Media and Audiences in India

The interplay between media and its audience is a pivotal element of media sociology, particularly in a diverse and intricate society such as India. Comprehending how audiences engage with, interpret, and react to media content yields significant insights into the influence of media on social attitudes, cultural identities, and public discourse. This section examines the interplay between media and audience in India, emphasising audience segmentation, media consumption trends, and the consequences for social engagement and cultural expression.

Varied Audience Demographics

India's extensive population is marked by its diversity in language, religion, caste, and socio-economic status. This diversity profoundly impacts media consumption trends. Diverse audience segments interact with distinct media forms based on their cultural contexts, preferences, and technological access. Urban audiences typically possess enhanced access to digital platforms and international content, whereas rural audiences tend to depend more on regional television channels and local newspapers. This segmentation underscores the necessity for media producers to be aware of their audience's cultural and social contexts to generate pertinent content.

Patterns of Media Consumption

The emergence of digital technologies has revolutionised media consumption in India. The increase in smartphones and accessible internet has resulted in a rise in online content consumption, especially among younger demographics. Streaming services, social media, and mobile applications have emerged as principal sources of entertainment and information. This transition has transformed conventional media hierarchies and contested the supremacy of established broadcasters and print media.

Furthermore, the proliferation of regional language content has addressed varied audience preferences, facilitating enhanced representation of local cultures and narratives. Platforms such as YouTube and regional streaming services have facilitated content creation that resonates with particular linguistic and cultural demographics, allowing audiences to interact with media that mirrors their identities.

Engagement of an Active Audience

In India, audiences are not simply passive consumers of media; they actively engage with and interpret media content. Social media platforms have enabled audience engagement by permitting comments, sharing, and critique of media messages. This interactivity cultivates a sense of community among viewers and empowers marginalised voices to contest prevailing narratives. Social media campaigns focused on social justice issues frequently gain momentum as users share their experiences and advocate for change, demonstrating the capacity for collective action.

The dynamics of audience engagement are intricate. Although social media offers a venue for varied perspectives, it can also exacerbate polarising narratives and disseminate misinformation. The rapid dissemination of information on these platforms can result in the propagation of falsehoods, exacerbating societal polarisation. Comprehending how audiences traverse this environment is essential for promoting informed public discourse.

Cultural Representation and Identity Development

Media significantly influences cultural representations and the formation of identity among audiences. The representation of diverse social groups in media content affects individual self-perception and perceptions of others. The portrayal of women in Indian cinema has progressed over time, mirroring shifting societal perceptions of gender roles. Earlier films frequently reinforced conventional stereotypes, whereas modern narratives increasingly feature robust female characters and varied experiences, thereby altering perceptions of gender identity.

Regional media is essential for the preservation and promotion of local cultures and languages. Regional television channels and print media frequently emphasise cultural events, festivals, and local issues, cultivating a sense of pride and identity among viewers. This localised content allows individuals to engage with their heritage and cultural origins, emphasising the significance of representation in media.

Summary

The relationship between media and audience in India is marked by complexity and dynamism. Diverse audience demographics, changing consumption patterns, and active interaction with media content influence the media landscape. As audiences confront the challenges and opportunities posed by digital technologies, comprehending their role in interpreting and responding to media messages is crucial. Acknowledging the influence of media on cultural representation and identity development emphasises the necessity for inclusive and diverse media narratives that reflect the varied Indian population.

The Influence of Mass Media on the Promotion of Nationalism, Regionalism, Secularism, Democracy, Social Justice, and Gender Sensitivity in India

Mass media in India serves a complex function in shaping societal values, influencing public opinion, and advancing diverse ideologies.

Considering India's diversity, the capacity of mass media to engage with nationalism, regionalism, secularism, democracy, social justice, and gender sensitivity is notably important. This section analyses the role of mass media in these essential facets of Indian society and its effects on social cohesion and cultural identity.

Nationalism and Mass Media

Mass media functions as a potent instrument for advancing nationalism in India by cultivating a sense of collective identity and common values. The media fosters a national identity that surpasses regional and cultural distinctions through patriotic programming, news coverage of national events, and the depiction of historical narratives. The portrayal of Independence Day festivities and national sports accomplishments frequently elicits pride and unity among audiences, strengthening their sense of belonging to the Indian nation.

Nevertheless, the advancement of nationalism via media may also result in exclusionary narratives that marginalise minority groups. Media portrayals that prioritise a singular national identity may neglect the diverse cultures and histories present in India. The challenge is to reconcile national pride with the acknowledgement of the country's pluralism, guaranteeing that all voices are included in the national narrative.

Regionalism and Local Media

The regional diversity of India requires the existence of regional media that addresses local cultures, languages, and concerns. Regional television channels, newspapers, and online platforms are essential in fostering regional identities and addressing local issues. This localised media environment facilitates the commemoration of regional festivals, languages, and cultural traditions, cultivating a sense of pride among audiences.

Nonetheless, regional media can also foster regionalism that occasionally approaches separatism. When local identities are prioritised over a national identity, there is a risk of intensifying regional tensions. Media outlets must manage the intricate equilibrium between encouraging regional pride and cultivating a sense of unity among the diverse populace.

Secularism and Mass Media

Secularism is a fundamental tenet of Indian democracy, highlighting the distinction between religious and governmental matters. Mass media is instrumental in advancing secularism by offering platforms for various religious perspectives and facilitating dialogue among disparate communities. Reporting on interfaith initiatives, religious festivals, and secular events promotes comprehension and acceptance among various religious communities.

The depiction of religious matters in the media may result in polarisation and communal discord. Exaggerated reporting on communal violence or religious conflicts can intensify divisions among communities. Media outlets must implement responsible reporting practices that emphasise accuracy and foster peaceful coexistence.

The Function of Media in a Democratic Society

Mass media is commonly designated as the "fourth estate" in a democratic society, functioning as a watchdog that ensures accountability of power and informs the populace. In India, mass media is essential for promoting democratic participation by informing citizens about government policies, political events, and social concerns. Investigative journalism and critical reporting are essential for fostering transparency and accountability in the political system.

Nonetheless, the media landscape in India encounters challenges, such as press freedom issues and the concentration of media ownership. Corporate interests and political affiliations may undermine journalistic integrity, resulting in biassed reporting and restricted access to diverse perspectives. To fortify democracy, it is essential to maintain the tenets of free and independent journalism.

Social Justice and Mass Media

Mass media can enhance the visibility of advocates for social justice and equality in India. The examination of issues like caste discrimination, gender violence, and environmental justice enhances awareness and galvanises public support for marginalised communities. Social movements and grassroots organisations frequently utilise media platforms to enhance their messages and promote policy reforms.

However, media portrayal of social justice issues can be contentious. Sensationalist reporting can simplify intricate social issues into superficial headlines, diminishing the complexities and personal experiences of those impacted. The media must endeavour to report responsibly, accurately portraying the realities of marginalised communities and advancing social justice.

Gender Sensitivity in Media Representation

The depiction of gender in Indian media has experienced substantial transformations, with a growing focus on gender sensitivity and representation. Media narratives that contest conventional gender roles and emphasise women's empowerment facilitate the transformation of societal attitudes regarding gender equality. Films, television programs, and advertisements that depict robust female characters and tackle issues such as gender-based violence contribute to raising awareness and facilitating discourse on gender matters.

Nevertheless, despite advancements, stereotypes and misogynistic representations endure in diverse media formats. The objectification of women and the reinforcement of patriarchal norms persist in specific genres, fostering detrimental societal attitudes. Media creators must emphasise gender sensitivity in their narratives, ensuring that diverse female experiences are represented and esteemed.

The Influence of Information Technology on Media in India

The emergence of information technology has significantly altered the media landscape in India, redefining the processes of content creation, distribution, and consumption. The emergence of the internet, coupled with the widespread adoption of smartphones and social media, has transformed the methods of information dissemination and access. This section analyses the influence of information technology on media in India, focussing on its effects on content creation, audience engagement, and the associated challenges.

The Digital Transformation in India

The digital revolution has instigated a substantial transformation in India's media landscape. The extensive accessibility of the internet and economical smartphones has democratised information access, allowing a broader segment of the populace to interact with diverse media forms. Recent statistics indicate that India possesses one of the largest online user bases globally, with millions of individuals engaging with digital content daily. This transition has resulted in the rise of new media platforms that contest the supremacy of traditional media, such as streaming services, social media networks, and news aggregators.

Content Generation and Dissemination

Information technology has enabled individuals and small media organisations to create and disseminate content more effectively. The emergence of user-generated content platforms, including YouTube and social media, has democratised content creation, enabling individuals from varied backgrounds to disseminate their narratives and viewpoints. This has resulted in an increase of voices in the media landscape, contesting conventional narratives and offering representation for marginalised communities.

Furthermore, the capacity to generate and distribute content instantaneously has enabled the swift propagation of information. Social media facilitates real-time reporting of news events, allowing citizens to engage in the news creation process. This transition has obscured the distinctions between media producers and consumers, promoting a more participatory media culture.

Audience Involvement and Interactivity

The influence of information technology on audience engagement is significant. Social media platforms enable audiences to engage with content creators, express their views, and partake in discussions regarding media narratives. This interactivity cultivates a sense of community and enables audiences to influence the discourse surrounding social issues. Campaigns promoting social justice or environmental sustainability frequently gain traction via social media, facilitating collective action and enhancing awareness.

Nonetheless, the interactivity provided by digital platforms also poses challenges. The emergence of echo chambers, wherein individuals encounter solely information that corroborates their preexisting convictions, can result in polarisation and misinformation. The rapid dissemination of information can lead to the propagation of false narratives, underscoring the necessity for media literacy among audiences to effectively navigate this intricate environment.

Obstacles of Regulation and Oversight

The swift proliferation of digital media prompts significant enquiries concerning regulation and oversight. The Indian government has enacted several measures to regulate online content, citing concerns regarding misinformation, hate speech, and national security. Although regulation is crucial for sustaining a robust media ecosystem, excessive oversight can inhibit free expression and restrict the diversity of perspectives within the media landscape.

The difficulty resides in achieving equilibrium between regulation and freedom of expression. Achieving this equilibrium necessitates a sophisticated comprehension of the digital environment and the varied viewpoints that influence it. Involving stakeholders from diverse sectors, such as civil society, media professionals, and technology experts, is crucial for formulating effective regulatory frameworks that safeguard public interests and individual rights.

The Function of Media Literacy

As information technology progressively influences the media landscape, media literacy is becoming more essential. Audiences must possess the ability to critically assess media content, differentiate credible sources from unreliable ones, and navigate the intricacies of the digital landscape. Media literacy programs that foster critical thinking and informed media consumption can enable individuals to interact meaningfully with media narratives.

Educational institutions, civil society organisations, and media entities are instrumental in advancing media literacy. Integrating media literacy programs into curricula and community outreach initiatives enables stakeholders to cultivate a more informed and engaged citizenry adept at navigating the challenges of the digital age.

Regulation and Oversight of Media in India

The regulation and oversight of media in India are pivotal matters that influence the framework of information distribution and public dialogue. India, as a democracy with a diverse and pluralistic society, faces the challenge of reconciling the necessity for regulation with the safeguarding of free speech and expression. This section analyses the mechanisms of media regulation in India, the challenges related to media control, and the consequences for democracy and social justice.

Historical Context of Media Regulation

The history of media regulation in India is characterised by pivotal events that have shaped the evolution of media policies. The Press Act of 1910 and the ensuing Press Commission reports instituted initial frameworks for media regulation under British colonial governance. Following independence, the Indian government implemented several statutes, such as the Press Council Act of 1978 and the Cable Television Networks (Regulation) Act of 1995, to govern print and electronic media.

Although the purpose of these regulations has frequently been to maintain journalistic integrity and safeguard public interest, they have simultaneously elicited apprehensions about censorship and governmental overreach. The Emergency period (1975-1977) exemplifies the potential for media suppression, as the government enforced stringent censorship on the press, resulting in a deterioration of press freedom.

Modern Regulatory Framework

In modern India, media regulation is managed by multiple entities, including the Ministry of Information and Broadcasting, the Telecom Regulatory Authority of India (TRAI), and the Press Council of India. These organisations are responsible for ensuring adherence to established standards, overseeing content, and resolving complaints concerning media practices.

The emergence of digital media has required the establishment of new regulatory frameworks to tackle issues related to online content. The Information Technology Act of 2000, along with its subsequent amendments, establishes regulations for digital platforms. The swift advancement of technology presents challenges for regulators as they endeavour to stay abreast of emerging trends and practices in the digital realm.

Obstacles of Censorship and Regulation

A primary challenge of media regulation in India is the intricate balance between preserving public order and protecting freedom of expression. Censorship, whether via formal mechanisms or informal pressures, raises concerns regarding the deterioration of press freedom. Journalists and media entities frequently encounter threats, intimidation, and legal obstacles when covering sensitive topics, including corruption, human rights violations, and governmental accountability.

Furthermore, the emergence of digital media has presented novel challenges concerning content regulation. The surge of disinformation, hate speech, and false narratives on social media has elicited demands for more stringent regulations. Excessive regulation can inhibit legitimate discourse and suppress dissenting voices, thereby undermining democratic principles.

The Function of Civil Society in Media Regulation

Civil society organisations and media advocacy groups are essential in fostering accountability and transparency in media regulation. They oversee media practices, champion press freedom, and promote awareness regarding censorship and media regulation issues. Efforts to safeguard journalists, enhance media literacy, and encourage responsible reporting are crucial for reinforcing democratic principles and ensuring the representation of diverse perspectives in the media sphere.

Public discourse regarding media regulation must encompass a diverse array of stakeholders, including journalists, policymakers, representatives of civil society, and media consumers. Participating in constructive discourse can result in more efficient regulatory frameworks that reconcile the necessity for oversight with the safeguarding of free expression.

The Prospects of Media Regulation in India

The future of media regulation in India necessitates a nuanced approach that accounts for the swift advancements in technology and evolving media consumption trends. Policymakers must manoeuvre through the intricacies of the digital realm while maintaining democratic ideals and safeguarding individual rights. This may entail cultivating cooperative regulatory strategies that involve various stakeholders and enhance transparency and accountability.

Moreover, investing in media literacy initiatives that enable audiences to critically analyse media content can alleviate the effects of misinformation and foster informed public discourse. By cultivating a media ecosystem that prioritises diversity, representation, and accountable journalism, India can reinforce its democratic principles and advance social justice.

Ethics of Media in India

Media ethics comprises the moral principles and standards that regulate journalism and media production practices. In India, characterised by a diverse and intricate media landscape, the significance of ethical journalism is paramount. This section examines the principal ethical considerations in Indian media, the obstacles encountered by journalists and media organisations, and the ramifications for public trust and accountability.

Comprehending Media Ethics

Media ethics encompasses a framework of principles that directs journalists and media professionals in their endeavours. Essential ethical considerations encompass accuracy, fairness, transparency, accountability, and the safeguarding of sources. Ethical journalism seeks to deliver precise and trustworthy information to the public, maintain individual dignity, and advance social justice.

The necessity for ethical standards in India is especially urgent given the diverse and frequently polarised media landscape. Journalists traverse intricate social dynamics and must reconcile the obligation to inform the public with the necessity to uphold individual rights and foster social cohesion.

Obstacles to Ethical Journalism

Notwithstanding the significance of media ethics, journalists in India encounter various challenges that undermine their capacity to uphold ethical standards. Influences from political bodies, corporate agendas, and societal norms can result in skewed reporting and the spread of misinformation. Journalists may encounter threats or reprisals for covering sensitive topics, such as corruption or human rights violations, resulting in self-censorship and hesitance to undertake investigative reporting.

Furthermore, the proliferation of sensationalism and clickbait culture in the digital era has exacerbated ethical dilemmas. The quest for viewership and engagement frequently supersedes ethical journalism, resulting in the prioritisation of sensational narratives over factual reporting. This transition diminishes public confidence in media organisations and exacerbates the decline of journalistic integrity.

The Function of Media Organisations in Advancing Ethical Standards

Media organisations play a vital role in advancing ethical journalism. Establishing stringent editorial policies, delivering training on media ethics, and cultivating a culture of accountability are crucial measures for maintaining ethical standards. Moreover, media organisations must establish secure environments that enable journalists to report without fear of retaliation.

Enhancing transparency in media operations is essential for fostering public trust. Disclosing ownership, funding sources, and editorial practices enables audiences to critically assess media content and recognise potential biases. By emphasising transparency and accountability, media organisations can bolster their credibility and reinforce their position as trustworthy sources of information.

The Influence of Social Media on Ethical Norms

The emergence of social media has revolutionised the media landscape, offering both prospects and obstacles for ethical journalism. Although social media platforms have democratised information dissemination and created new opportunities for engagement, they have also enabled the swift proliferation of misinformation and false news. Journalists must navigate a complex landscape shaped by social media, where ethical considerations are paramount.

Media organisations must modify their practices to confront the distinct challenges of the digital era. This entails the implementation of fact-checking protocols, the promotion of media literacy among audiences, and the engagement in responsible reporting practices. By cultivating an ethical culture that encompasses digital platforms, media organisations can enhance public awareness and engagement.

The Prospects of Media Ethics in India

The future of media ethics in India necessitates continuous reflection and adaptation. As the media landscape evolves, journalists and media organisations must remain dedicated to maintaining ethical standards while addressing emerging challenges. Interacting with audiences, civil society, and media specialists can promote a more inclusive methodology in ethical journalism.

Enhancing media literacy and critical engagement among audiences is crucial for cultivating a more informed populace. Equipping individuals with the ability to critically assess media content enables society to reduce the influence of misinformation and bolster public confidence in media institutions.

In summary, media ethics is essential in influencing journalistic practices in India. Despite the challenges presented by political pressures, sensationalism, and the proliferation of digital media, adherence to ethical standards is crucial for cultivating public trust and accountability. By emphasising accuracy, equity, and transparency, journalists and media entities can enhance a media environment that fosters social justice, educates the public, and sustains democratic principles.

MEDIA AND LAWS

The media laws in India form a complex framework that governs the operation of diverse media types, including print, broadcast, and digital platforms. This legal framework is crucial for safeguarding freedom of expression while concurrently addressing the responsibilities and liabilities of media professionals. As the media landscape transforms, the corresponding laws also adapt, mirroring shifts in technology, society, and politics. This section examines the principal elements of media legislation in India, encompassing their historical evolution, contemporary regulations, and the challenges posed by a swiftly transforming media landscape.

Contextual History

The genesis of media legislation in India can be traced to the British colonial era, characterised by stringent regulations and censorship of the press. The Indian Press Act of 1910 represented an early effort by the British government to regulate the press, imposing severe penalties on publishers and mandating their registration with the government. This action encountered significant opposition from Indian journalists and freedom fighters, who perceived it as a violation of their right to free expression.

Following independence, the Indian Constitution, enacted in 1950, established the framework for media legislation in the nation. Article 19(1)(a) ensures the right to freedom of speech and expression, establishing the legal foundation for a free press. This right is not absolute; it is subject to reasonable limitations as outlined in Article 19(2), which encompasses factors such as security, defamation, and public order. The equilibrium between liberty and regulation continues to be a pivotal aspect in the development of media legislation in India.

Media and the IPC (Indian Penal Code)

The Indian Penal Code (IPC) contains several provisions that impact media operations. Key sections include:

Defamation (Section 499-502): Defamation laws protect individuals from false statements that harm their reputation. Media organizations must exercise caution when publishing content to avoid defamation claims. The burden of proof lies with the accused, who must demonstrate that their statements were true and made in the public interest.

Sedation (Section 124A): The sedition law criminalizes actions that incite hatred or contempt against the government. This provision has often been criticized for being misused to silence dissent and curb journalistic freedom. High-profile cases, such as the arrest of journalists and activists for alleged sedition, have sparked widespread debate about its implications for free speech.

Hate Speech (Section 153A): This section penalizes acts that promote enmity between different religious or ethnic groups. In the context of media, the dissemination of hate speech through various platforms raises ethical and legal concerns about accountability and responsibility.

Media and the CrPC (Criminal Procedure Code)

The Criminal Procedure Code (CrPC) complements the IPC by outlining the procedures for the investigation and prosecution of offenses, including those related to media operations. Essential elements comprise:

The CrPC permits media coverage of court proceedings, thereby enhancing transparency in the judicial process. Nonetheless, the media must comply with ethical standards to prevent biassing ongoing trials or shaping public opinion.

The right to a fair trial may be influenced by media coverage. Judicial authorities frequently impose gag orders to limit media coverage of sensitive cases, thereby safeguarding impartiality and fairness in the legal proceedings.

The media significantly influences the dissemination of information regarding arrests and bail proceedings. This may result in sensationalism and conjecture, necessitating demands for responsible journalism that honours individuals' rights and reputations.

Self-Regulation

Self-regulation is an essential element of media legislation in India, especially within the print and broadcast industries. Numerous industry organisations have been created to advocate for ethical standards and optimal practices among media professionals.

The Press Council of India (PCI), established in 1966, seeks to uphold press freedom while ensuring accountability. It examines grievances regarding the media and proposes strategies to enhance journalistic standards. The PCI's guidelines underscore veracity, precision, and equity in reporting.

The Broadcasting Content Complaints Council (BCCC) functions as a self-regulatory entity for the television sector, managing viewer grievances regarding content. Its objective is to foster responsible broadcasting through the establishment of standards and guidelines for programming.

The Ministry of Information and Broadcasting has issued guidelines for digital media in response to the increasing influence of online platforms, emphasising transparency, accountability, and ethical reporting.

Print Media and the Genesis of the 'Press Laws'

The development of print media legislation in India originates from colonial regulations designed to stifle dissent. The Press Act of 1910 and ensuing legislation established the foundation for contemporary press laws. Significant advancements encompass:

The Press and Registration of Books Act, 1867 mandated that printers and publishers register their establishments with the government. It sought to regulate the dissemination of information and guarantee accountability.

The Freedom of the Press: Following independence, the press became an essential institution for democracy, significantly influencing public discourse. The Supreme Court has underscored the significance of press freedom in pivotal rulings, highlighting its function as a guardian of democracy.

Modern press legislation encompasses matters such as media ownership, transparency, and the safeguarding of journalistic sources. The Right to Information (RTI) Act of 2005 has enabled citizens to request information from public authorities, thereby augmenting accountability in government and media.

Broadcast Media: Development and Policy Challenges

The broadcast media in India has experienced substantial transformations since its inception. Significant advancements encompass:

The inception of Doordarshan in 1959 signified the commencement of public broadcasting in India. The television landscape, originally a government monopoly, expanded in the 1990s with the introduction of private channels, resulting in an increase in content and diversity of perspectives.

The Ministry of Information and Broadcasting governs broadcast media, overseeing content regulation, licensing, and adherence to ethical standards. The Broadcasting Regulatory Authority of India (BRAI) has been suggested to improve regulatory supervision.

Broadcast media encounters difficulties pertaining to sensationalism, commercialisation, and the indistinction between news and entertainment. The emergence of 24-hour news networks has heightened competition, prioritising ratings over ethical journalism. The media's influence on public perceptions and its obligation to report with accuracy and ethics are paramount issues.

Internet and the Contemporary Media Policy

The swift expansion of digital media has altered the media landscape in India, requiring new policies and regulations. Essential elements comprise:

The Ministry of Electronics and Information Technology (MeitY) governs the regulation of digital platforms. The Information Technology Act of 2000 establishes a legal framework for managing matters concerning online content, privacy, and cybersecurity.

The Digital Media Ethics Code seeks to establish guidelines for online content creators, fostering responsible reporting and safeguarding user rights.

The dynamic characteristics of the internet pose regulatory challenges. Challenges like online harassment, misinformation, and hate speech necessitate a sophisticated strategy to safeguard user safety while preserving freedom of expression.

Legislation Pertaining to Media and Gender

Media legislation in India intersects with gender issues, particularly regarding representation and rights. Essential factors to consider are:
Media representations of women frequently mirror societal biases and stereotypes. Ethical media practices ought to foster diverse and affirmative representations that empower women and contest gender norms.

Safety and Privacy: Female journalists encounter distinct challenges, encompassing harassment and threats. Media organisations must prioritise employee safety and implement policies to combat gender-based violence and discrimination.

The media is instrumental in promoting women's rights and social justice. By emphasising issues such as gender-based violence, discrimination, and inequality, media can facilitate societal change and enhance awareness of women's issues.

Media, the Indian Penal Code (IPC), and the Criminal Procedure Code (CrPC)

The Indian Penal Code (IPC) and the Criminal Procedure Code (CrPC) are essential elements of the legal framework regulating media activities in India. These codes delineate the legal parameters within which media professionals must function, reconciling the right to freedom of expression with the necessity of safeguarding individuals and society from harm. This section examines the particular stipulations of the IPC and CrPC that influence media practices, analysing their ramifications for journalists, content creators, and the public.

The Indian Penal Code, established in 1860, constitutes the foundation of criminal law in India. It delineates numerous offences and their associated penalties, including those pertinent to media operations. Crucial provisions of the IPC that overlap with media legislation encompass:

Defamation (Sections 499-502): Defamation statutes safeguard individuals against false assertions that damage their reputation. Media professionals must manoeuvre through the intricacies of defamation when reporting on individuals or organisations. The onus of proof rests with the accused, necessitating that they establish the veracity of their statements and their alignment with the public interest.

Case Study: Prominent defamation cases, particularly those concerning public figures, exemplify the difficulties journalists encounter in reconciling the public's right to information with individuals' rights to safeguard their reputation. A celebrity litigating a media organisation for defamation may lead to protracted legal disputes that underscore the fragile balance between press freedom and personal rights.

Sedition (Section 124A): Sedition laws penalise actions that provoke animosity or disdain towards the government. This provision has frequently faced criticism for its misuse to suppress dissent and restrict journalistic freedom. Journalists and activists have been charged with sedition for reporting on governmental policies or participating in protests, which raises concerns regarding the chilling effect on free expression.

The apprehension of journalists on sedition charges for their coverage of anti-government protests highlights the conflict between governmental authority and press liberty. Such instances have ignited extensive discourse regarding the suitability and constitutionality of sedition statutes within a democratic framework.

Hate Speech (Section 153A): This section penalises actions that incite animosity between various religious or ethnic groups. The propagation of hate speech across diverse media platforms engenders ethical and legal dilemmas regarding accountability and responsibility.

Case Study: The proliferation of communal hate speech during electoral campaigns has elicited demands for more stringent regulations on media content. Prominent instances of hate speech in news broadcasts or social media demonstrate the capacity of media to intensify societal tensions, highlighting the need for meticulous evaluation of media's role in fostering harmony and averting conflict.

Ethical Considerations: Journalists must balance the obligation to report on legal proceedings with the necessity of upholding defendants' right to a fair trial. Excessive media coverage of prominent trials can erode public trust in the judiciary and the integrity of the legal system.

The right to a fair trial may be influenced by media coverage. Judicial authorities frequently impose gag orders to limit media coverage of sensitive cases, thereby safeguarding impartiality and fairness in the legal proceedings.

Case Study: Prominent criminal cases, particularly those involving politicians or celebrities, frequently garner extensive media attention. Courts may impose gag orders to avert prejudicial reporting that could sway jurors or public perception, underscoring the tenuous equilibrium between press liberty and the integrity of the judicial system.

The media significantly influences the dissemination of information regarding arrests and bail proceedings. This may result in sensationalism and conjecture, necessitating demands for responsible journalism that honours individuals' rights and reputations.

The challenges of sensationalism include the phenomenon of trial by media, wherein sensational reporting of arrests influences public opinion prior to a fair legal process. Journalists must endeavour to report with responsibility and ethics, eschewing speculation and guaranteeing accuracy in their coverage.

Self-Regulation in Media

Self-regulation is a crucial component of media ethics and accountability in India. Numerous industry associations and organisations have been created to advocate for ethical standards and optimal practices among media professionals.

The Press Council of India (PCI): Founded in 1966, the PCI seeks to uphold press freedom while guaranteeing accountability. It examines grievances against the media and proposes strategies to enhance journalistic standards. The PCI's guidelines underscore veracity, precision, and equity in reporting.

The PCI is essential for upholding press integrity by addressing public complaints and fostering ethical standards among journalists. Its recommendations and rulings promote a culture of accountability within the media sector.

The Broadcasting Content Complaints Council (BCCC) functions as a self-regulatory entity for the television sector, managing viewer grievances regarding content. It seeks to advance responsible broadcasting by establishing standards and guidelines for programming.

Challenges of Self-Regulation: Although self-regulatory bodies endeavour to maintain ethical standards, difficulties persist in guaranteeing adherence among media organisations. The efficacy of self-regulation hinges on the commitment of media organisations to comply with established protocols and maintain accountability.

The Ministry of Information and Broadcasting promulgated guidelines for digital media to enhance transparency, accountability, and ethical reporting in light of the increasing impact of online platforms.

The Digital Age's Impact: The emergence of digital media has revolutionised the media landscape, requiring innovative methods of self-regulation. Ethical dilemmas concerning misinformation, hate speech, and online harassment necessitate proactive interventions from digital content creators and platforms.

Ethics and Accountability in Media

The convergence of media legislation, ethics, and accountability is essential for preserving public confidence in media organisations. Essential factors to consider are:

Ethical Reporting: Media professionals must prioritise ethical reporting by ensuring accuracy, fairness, and respect for individual rights. Compliance with ethical standards enhances public trust in the media as a reliable information source.

Accountability Mechanisms: Implementing accountability mechanisms, including independent regulatory entities and comprehensive complaint procedures, augments the media's obligation to the public. These mechanisms allow individuals to pursue remedies for grievances concerning media content.

The media's reputation is influenced by its compliance with ethical standards and the legal regulations that govern its activities. Maintaining journalistic integrity is crucial for preserving public trust and credibility.

Self-Regulation: Print Media and the Genesis of the 'Press Laws'

Self-regulation in the print media industry is essential for maintaining ethical journalism and accountability. The origins of press laws in India, fundamentally grounded in the historical context of colonial governance, have developed to influence modern self-regulatory practices. This section analyses the historical evolution of press legislation, the function of self-regulation in fostering ethical standards, and the obstacles encountered by the print media sector in upholding accountability.

Historical Context of Press Legislation

The genesis of press laws in India can be traced to the colonial period, during which stringent regulations were enacted to regulate the dissemination of information and stifle dissent. Significant advancements encompass:

The Press Act of 1910 sought to regulate the press and restrict freedom of expression. It mandated that publishers register with the government, instituted severe penalties for non-compliance, and permitted authorities to confiscate printing presses. The action encountered considerable opposition from journalists and activists, who perceived it as a violation of their rights.

The Press Act's repressive characteristics motivated journalists and activists to champion press freedom, establishing the foundation for a free press in post-independence India.

Post-Independence Developments: After India's independence in 1947, the architects of the Constitution acknowledged the significance of a free press in a democratic society. Article 19(1)(a) ensures the right to freedom of speech and expression, establishing the constitutional foundation for a free press.

The Press Council of India (PCI) was established in 1966 as a self-regulatory entity to advocate for and maintain press freedom while ensuring accountability. The PCI addresses grievances regarding the press, establishes guidelines, and promotes ethical journalism.

The Function of Self-Regulation

Self-regulation is essential for upholding ethical standards in the print media sector. Essential elements comprise:

The PCI and other industry organisations formulate ethical guidelines that delineate standards for responsible journalism. These guidelines underscore veracity, precision, equity, and respect for individual rights.

The significance of ethics: Upholding ethical standards is crucial for preserving public confidence in the media. Journalists must traverse the intricacies of reporting, balancing the public's right to information with the obligation to prevent harm.

The PCI establishes a framework for addressing public complaints concerning media content. This mechanism enables individuals to pursue redress for grievances and fosters accountability within the media sector.

Compliance Challenges: Although self-regulation seeks to improve accountability, difficulties persist in guaranteeing adherence among media organisations. The efficacy of self-regulation relies on the commitment of media organisations to comply with established protocols and maintain accountability.

Media organisations must prioritise the training and education of journalists to foster ethical reporting practices. Ongoing professional development assists journalists in manoeuvring through the changing media environment and confronting new ethical dilemmas.

Press Legislation and Its Consequences

The development of press legislation in India has considerable consequences for the operation of the print media sector. Essential elements comprise:

The equilibrium between freedom of expression and regulation continues to be a pivotal issue in press legislation. The Constitution ensures the right to freedom of speech, yet this right is subject to reasonable limitations intended to safeguard public order, morality, and individual rights.

Case Studies: Pivotal Supreme Court rulings have underscored the significance of press freedom while highlighting the necessity for responsible journalism. Cases pertaining to defamation, sedition, and hate speech underscore the intricacies of traversing legal parameters in journalism.

The emergence of digital media has revolutionised the print media sector, presenting novel challenges for both regulation and self-regulation. Traditional print media must evolve to meet the demands of the digital era, confronting challenges associated with online content, misinformation, and the indistinction between news and opinion.

The rise of new media: The expansion of social media platforms has democratised the distribution of information, allowing individuals to assume the role of content creators. This transition prompts enquiries regarding accountability and the function of self-regulation in the digital realm.

Press legislation must tackle matters of representation and diversity in the media. Incorporating diverse voices and perspectives in reporting is crucial for advancing social justice and inclusivity.

Obstacles to Self-Regulation

Notwithstanding the implementation of self-regulatory mechanisms, the print media sector encounters numerous challenges:

Sensationalism and Commercialisation: The quest for ratings and profit may result in sensational reporting that favours entertainment over ethical journalism. This trend elicits apprehensions regarding the integrity of information and the media's influence on public discourse. Countering Sensationalism: Media entities must refrain from the allure of sensationalising news for financial profit. Ethical reporting practices should supersede profit motives to maintain the integrity of journalism. The swift dissemination of misinformation and fake news presents considerable obstacles to self-regulation. Print media must formulate strategies to counter misinformation while upholding transparency and accountability.

The Role of Fact-Checking: Establishing comprehensive fact-checking systems and enhancing media literacy among audiences can mitigate misinformation and reinstate public confidence in the media.

Governmental Pressure: Journalists frequently encounter pressure from authorities, resulting in self-censorship and a compromise of journalistic integrity. Addressing this pressure necessitates a dedication to ethical journalism and a readiness to champion press freedom.

Broadcast Media: Development and Policy Challenges

The evolution of broadcast media in India has profoundly altered the media landscape, impacting public opinion, shaping culture, and enhancing democratic discourse. With the evolution of broadcast media, the policies and regulations governing its operations have also transformed. This section analyses the historical evolution of broadcast media in India, the regulatory framework governing its operations, and the challenges encountered by the industry in adapting to a swiftly transforming media landscape.

Historical Context of Broadcasting Media

Broadcast media in India has experienced substantial transformations since its inception. Significant advancements encompass:

The inception of broadcasting in India occurred in 1923 with the formation of the Indian Broadcasting Company. Radio rapidly emerged as an essential medium for the transmission of information, entertainment, and education.

Government Regulation: Broadcasting was initially regulated by the government, culminating in the establishment of All India Radio (AIR) in 1936 as a public service broadcaster. This broadcasting monopoly persisted for decades, constraining competition and programming diversity.

The Television Era: The inception of Doordarshan in 1959 signified the commencement of public television broadcasting. Originally a government monopoly, Doordarshan concentrated on educational and informational content.

The liberalisation of the Indian economy in the 1990s facilitated the emergence of private television channels, leading to an abundance of content and heightened competition. This transition represented a pivotal moment in the broadcast media landscape, as private channels started to prevail in viewership.

Regulatory Structure for Broadcast Media

The regulatory framework for broadcast media in India consists of multiple laws and authorities that supervise content, licensing, and adherence to regulations. Essential elements comprise:

The Ministry of Information and Broadcasting supervises broadcast media, regulating content, licensing, and adherence to ethical standards. It is instrumental in formulating broadcast policy and ensuring compliance with established regulations.

The licensing framework for private broadcasters has developed, with the government issuing licenses for television channel operation contingent upon adherence to content and technical standards.

The proposed Broadcasting Regulatory Authority of India (BRAI) seeks to augment regulatory supervision of the broadcasting industry. It aims to tackle matters concerning content regulation, pricing, and consumer protection.

Regulatory Challenges: Despite the efforts of regulatory bodies to uphold standards, difficulties persist in ensuring compliance among broadcasters. The efficacy of regulation relies on the readiness of media organisations to comply with established standards and maintain accountability.

The regulatory framework encompasses guidelines for content regulation, tackling issues such as obscenity, hate speech, and misinformation. Broadcasters must comply with these guidelines to ensure responsible broadcasting.

Establishing ethical standards for programming is crucial to uphold public trust in broadcast media. Broadcasters must emphasise precision, impartiality, and respect for individual rights in their reporting.

Obstacles Encountered by Broadcast Media

As broadcast media evolves, it encounters numerous challenges that affect its operation and credibility:

Sensationalism and Commercialisation: The quest for ratings and profit may result in sensational reporting that favours entertainment over ethical journalism. This trend prompts apprehensions regarding the integrity of information and the media's influence on public discourse.

Case Study: The emergence of 24-hour news channels has heightened competition, resulting in sensationalised reporting of breaking news.

Journalists must balance the demands of ratings-oriented reporting with the maintenance of ethical standards.

Digital Disruption: The emergence of digital media has revolutionised the broadcasting sector, presenting novel challenges for conventional broadcasters. Streaming platforms, social media, and online news outlets have transformed audience consumption behaviours and intensified competition for viewership.

Adaptation Strategies: Broadcasters must acclimatise to the digital era by adopting new technologies and investigating novel content distribution methods. This may involve creating online platforms, interacting with audiences via social media, and diversifying programming to accommodate evolving preferences.

Regulatory Challenges: The changing media landscape presents difficulties for regulatory authorities in adapting to technological progress. Achieving compliance with content regulations while promoting innovation necessitates a sophisticated strategy.

The involvement of stakeholders, such as government entities, industry organisations, and civil society, is crucial for formulating regulatory frameworks that harmonise innovation with accountability.

Representation and Diversity in Broadcast Media
The inclusion of varied voices and perspectives in broadcast media is essential for advancing social justice and inclusivity. Essential factors to consider are:

Content Diversity: Broadcast media must endeavour to represent varied communities and perspectives, guaranteeing that marginalised voices are acknowledged. This encompasses tackling issues related to gender, caste, religion, and socio-economic status in programming.
Diverse representation in broadcast media influences public perceptions and contests stereotypes. By advancing inclusive narratives, broadcasters can cultivate understanding and dialogue among diverse communities.

Gender Representation: The representation of women in broadcast media continues to be a significant concern. Despite advancements in journalism, women continue to face challenges concerning bias, harassment, and under-representation.

Advancing Gender Equity: Broadcasters should prioritise gender equity in recruitment, programming, and content representation. Advocating for women journalists and tackling gender-based violence in media is crucial for cultivating a more inclusive media landscape.

Internet and New Media Policy

The emergence of the internet has transformed the media landscape, leading to novel modes of communication, content generation, and information distribution. With the expansion of digital media's influence, the necessity for comprehensive new media policies has become increasingly critical. This section analyses the development of internet and new media policies in India, the regulatory frameworks overseeing online content, and the challenges encountered in ensuring accountability and fostering ethical standards in the digital realm.

The Development of New Media in India

The advent of new media in India originated in the late 1990s, coinciding with the increased accessibility of the internet to the general populace. Significant advancements encompass:

The Internet Boom: The liberalisation of the Indian economy in the 1990s facilitated the expansion of internet services. The advent of economical internet access and mobile technology resulted in a proliferation of online content creation and consumption.

The proliferation of social media platforms like Facebook, Twitter, and WhatsApp has revolutionised interpersonal communication and information dissemination. These platforms have evolved into formidable instruments for expression, activism, and community development.

The rise of digital news platforms has democratised information dissemination, allowing a variety of voices to participate in public discourse. Online journalism has proliferated as conventional media outlets adjust to the digital era.

Credibility Challenges: Although digital platforms have enhanced information accessibility, they simultaneously provoke concerns regarding credibility, misinformation, and reporting quality. The simplicity of disseminating information online can result in the swift proliferation of false narratives.

Regulatory Structure for Emerging Media

The regulatory framework for new media in India consists of multiple laws and policies that pertain to online content, privacy, and cybersecurity. Essential elements comprise:

The Information Technology Act of 2000 establishes the legal framework for the regulation of online content and the mitigation of cybercrime. It encompasses stipulations for the safeguarding of personal data, intermediary liability, and the governance of electronic commerce.

The IT Act substantially influences digital media by regulating the liability of platforms concerning user-generated content. Although it seeks to encourage responsible online conduct, difficulties persist in ensuring adherence.

The government has released directives for content regulation on digital platforms, focussing on concerns such as hate speech, misinformation, and online harassment. These guidelines aim to foster responsible content moderation while maintaining freedom of expression.

The enforcement of content regulations presents challenges due to the extensive nature of the internet, which complicates the effective monitoring and regulation of all online content. Cooperation among stakeholders is crucial for ensuring compliance and fostering accountability.

The necessity for stringent data protection policies has become increasingly significant in the digital era. The proposed Personal Data Protection Bill aims to create a framework for safeguarding personal data, augmenting individual rights and encouraging responsible data practices.

Reconciling Privacy and Free Speech: Achieving equilibrium between safeguarding personal data and maintaining freedom of expression presents a multifaceted challenge. Policymakers must address the ramifications of data privacy on journalism and public discourse.

Obstacles Encountered by New Media

The emergence of new media poses numerous challenges that affect its operation and accountability:

The swift dissemination of misinformation and fake news presents considerable challenges for new media. The simplicity of content sharing on social media can result in the propagation of false narratives, affecting public perception and trust in media.

Addressing Misinformation: Establishing effective fact-checking systems and enhancing media literacy among audiences can mitigate misinformation and reinstate public confidence in digital media.

Regulatory Challenges: The dynamic evolution of digital media presents difficulties for regulatory agencies in maintaining alignment with technological progress. Achieving compliance with content regulations while promoting innovation necessitates a sophisticated strategy.

Collaboration among stakeholders, including government, industry, and civil society, is crucial for formulating effective regulatory frameworks that reconcile innovation with accountability.

The anonymity provided by the internet can result in online harassment and cyberbullying, adversely affecting individuals' rights and freedoms. Resolving these issues necessitates a comprehensive strategy, encompassing legal interventions, awareness initiatives, and support frameworks.

Advocating for Secure Online Environments: Ensuring secure online environments for individuals, especially marginalised groups, is essential for cultivating a healthy digital ecosystem. Platforms must prioritise user safety and implement measures to prevent harassment and abuse.

The emergence of the internet and new media has revolutionised the media landscape in India, offering opportunities for varied voices and content production. Nonetheless, it has also presented considerable challenges concerning misinformation, regulatory adherence, and online safety. Formulating extensive new media policies that encourage accountability, uphold ethical standards, and safeguard individuals' rights is crucial for cultivating a robust digital ecosystem. By tackling these challenges, policymakers can augment the function of new media in fostering democratic dialogue and empowering citizens in the digital era.

CHAPTER IV

MEDIA AND SOCIETY: PRACTICE

The Comprehending Media Content Production

In the digital era, media content creation has become an essential aspect of daily life. Individuals and organisations are increasingly involved in the creation and distribution of media content, ranging from social media posts and YouTube videos to podcasts and blog articles. This phenomenon reflects both technological advancements and the evolving dynamics of communication in modern society. Media content creation involves various activities focused on generating and disseminating information, entertainment, and artistic expression. Examining this process from a sociological perspective enables us to investigate its ramifications for society, culture, and personal identity.

The Sociological Context of Media Production

The creation of media content is shaped by numerous sociocultural factors, such as social norms, power dynamics, and cultural contexts. Individuals produce and disseminate media within a context influenced by their social surroundings, identities, and values. The sociological perspective underscores that media functions not only as a communication instrument but also as a social process capable of reinforcing or contesting societal norms.

Societal Norms and Expectations

Social norms govern the permissible methods by which individuals may articulate themselves via media. These norms can differ significantly depending on factors such as age, gender, ethnicity, and social class. The content that receives acclaim or condemnation frequently mirrors overarching societal values and expectations.

In numerous societies, there exist normative expectations regarding what is deemed "appropriate" content for particular platforms. Instagram prioritises aesthetics, prompting users to share visually captivating images, whereas Twitter's character restriction fosters conciseness and immediacy. These platform-specific conventions influence content creation and reception, frequently compelling creators to adhere to established styles and trends.

Power Dynamics in Media Production

The sociological perspective elucidates the power dynamics intrinsic to media content creation. Historically, traditional media has been monopolised by a limited number of major corporations and gatekeepers who regulated the dissemination of information. Nonetheless, the emergence of digital platforms has democratised media production, enabling individuals to establish themselves as content creators.

This transition has both advantageous and disadvantageous consequences. It empowers marginalised voices and offers a platform for diverse perspectives. Conversely, it may result in the continuation of misinformation and the spread of detrimental content. Comprehending these power dynamics is essential for creators as they traverse the media landscape and endeavour to amplify their voices.

The Procedure of Media Content Production

Media content creation encompasses multiple phases, ranging from conceptualisation to distribution. Every phase is influenced by societal factors, technological instruments, and personal ingenuity.

Conceptualisation and Ideation

The initial phase of media content creation is conceptualisation, during which the creator formulates an idea for their content. This phase is frequently shaped by individual preferences, prevailing trends, and audience anticipations. A content creator may derive inspiration from social issues, pop culture phenomena, or personal experiences, thereby reflecting their identity and values.

This stage is significant sociologically as it underscores the manner in which creators interact with their social milieu. The concepts they opt to investigate are frequently shaped by the cultural narratives and discourses dominant in society. The interplay between individual creativity and societal influences determines the themes and messages of the produced content.

Manufacturing

Upon the solidification of the concept, the production phase commences. This entails the production of media content, including video filming, podcast recording, article writing, or graphic design. At this stage, creators utilise diverse tools and technologies to actualise their concepts.

Production is not solely a technical procedure; it is also a cooperative endeavour. Numerous creators engage in collaborative efforts, either through informal associations or formal partnerships. This collaborative element underscores the significance of community and social networks in media production, wherein skills and resources are exchanged to improve the quality of the generated content.

Dissemination and Allocation

Once the content is produced, it must be disseminated to reach its target audience. The emergence of social media and online platforms has revolutionised the distribution process, enabling creators to disseminate their work broadly and instantaneously. This accessibility has facilitated the emergence of new audiences and communities, allowing creators to engage with individuals who possess analogous interests and values.

Nonetheless, distribution also prompts enquiries regarding visibility and acknowledgement. Digital platforms offer exposure opportunities but also establish a competitive environment where creators must manage algorithms, audience interaction, and content marketing. Comprehending the intricacies of distribution is essential for creators aiming to enhance their messages and expand their audiences.

The Influence of Audience in Media Content Production

The relationship between creators and audiences is a dynamic and interactive process that influences media content. Audience engagement can manifest in multiple ways, such as feedback, sharing, and involvement in content creation. This interaction is especially evident in the digital era, where audiences can directly engage with creators and impact the content being generated.

Audience Response

Historically, audience feedback was frequently restricted to formal critiques or evaluations. Currently, digital platforms facilitate instantaneous feedback, permitting creators to address comments, critiques, and suggestions from their audiences. This direct engagement can guide future content strategies, as creators modify their work to correspond with audience inclinations.

From a sociological standpoint, audience feedback signifies the dynamic character of communication within a participatory culture. Audiences have transitioned from passive consumers to active participants, influencing the media content they experience. This participatory model cultivates a sense of community and connection between creators and their audiences.

Cooperative Development

Alongside feedback, numerous creators encourage their audiences to engage in the content creation process. This collaborative method can manifest in diverse ways, including crowd-sourced projects, fan art, or community-driven initiatives. By engaging audiences in the creative process, creators can cultivate deeper connections and instill a sense of ownership among their followers.

Collaboration challenges conventional concepts of authorship and ownership in media production. It obscures the distinction between creator and audience, emphasising the collaborative essence of media production in the digital era. This sociological transformation signifies wider alterations in our comprehension of creativity and societal contribution.

The Significance of Media Content

Media content fulfils various functions: it informs, entertains, educates, and persuades. It can underscore social issues, commemorate culture, or mirror personal narratives. Comprehending the importance of the generated content is crucial. The media possesses the capacity to shape perceptions and influence societal norms, rendering it essential for creators to approach their work with deliberation.

CATEGORIES OF MEDIA CONTENT

Brief Cinematic Works:
These are generally narrative-focused and can vary in duration from a few seconds to approximately 30 minutes. The short film format

promotes succinct storytelling, enabling creators to swiftly examine themes, characters, and emotions.

Documentaries:

Documentaries aim to convey factual information, frequently examining social issues, personal narratives, or historical occurrences. They necessitate comprehensive research and frequently incorporate interviews, visual data, and a captivating narrative framework to engage the audience.

Periodicals:

Magazine content frequently amalgamates articles, essays, and visual components such as photography and illustrations. They cater to specialised markets or wider audiences and can encompass subjects ranging from lifestyle and fashion to politics and science.

Alternative Publications:

These publications frequently seek to convey perspectives and narratives overlooked by mainstream media. They function as platforms for marginalised voices and can contest prevailing narratives.

Weblogs (Blogs):

Blogs may encompass personal reflections, professional insights, and virtually any subject matter. They promote interaction and community involvement via comments and shares, rendering them dynamic content platforms.

PROCEDURES FOR DEVELOPING MEDIA CONTENT

Conceptual Development:

This preliminary phase entails generating ideas and determining the content's objective. Comprehending the target audience and the intended message is essential for crafting the content.

Pre-Production:

This phase encompasses research, script development, and logistical planning. In filmmaking, storyboarding is employed to visualise scenes, whereas magazine writers create outlines for articles to guarantee clarity and coherence.

Manufacturing:

This phase involves the creation of the actual content. In film, this entails capturing footage, whereas in writing, it includes composing articles or creating magazine layouts.

Post-Production:

For films, this encompasses editing footage, incorporating sound and visual effects, and producing a final cut. This entails proofreading, designing the layout, and preparing for publication in written media.

Allocation:

This entails determining the method of distributing the finalised work. Available options comprise film festivals, digital platforms, print distribution, or social media.

Ethical Considerations

The production of media content entails ethical obligations. It is essential to consider issues like representation, accuracy, and the potential impact of the content on audiences. Creators should strive for authenticity, avoid stereotypes, and ensure that marginalized voices are represented fairly. This involves ethical research practices and a commitment to truthfulness in storytelling.

Practical Activities

Group Projects:

Participants can form groups to create short films or documentaries on local issues or themes. This fosters Collaboration and allows participants to learn from each other's strengths.

Individual Assignments:

Participants can produce their own articles for a mock magazine or blog. This helps them develop their writing and storytelling skills.

Workshops:

Conduct workshops focusing on specific skills, such as film editing, scriptwriting, or magazine layout design. Hands-on practice reinforces learning.

Peer Evaluation Sessions:
Motivate participants to showcase their work to colleagues for constructive critique. This process enhances concepts and elevates the quality of the content.

Final Assessment

The creation of media content is a complex process shaped by social, cultural, and technological influences. Analysing this phenomenon from a sociological perspective enhances our comprehension of the dynamics influencing media creation and consumption. The relationship between creators and audiences, from idea conceptualisation to content distribution, underscores the significance of context, power dynamics, and community involvement.

Individuals involved in media content creation partake in a social process that both reflects and shapes their surrounding environment. By cultivating an understanding of these dynamics, we can enable creators to generate significant content that resonates with their audiences and contributes to the ongoing dialogues shaping our society. Ultimately, media content creation transcends mere information or entertainment production; it serves as a potent vehicle for identity expression, norm challenging, and connection fostering in an increasingly interconnected world.

MEDIA APPRECIATION: COMPREHENDING AND INTERACTING WITH MEDIA

In an era where media permeates all facets of our existence, from the news we engage with to the entertainment we enjoy, cultivating a sophisticated understanding of media is imperative. Media appreciation entails active engagement with media content, taking into account its aesthetic, cultural, and social implications rather than mere passive consumption. This thorough comprehension promotes critical analysis, improves personal articulation, and cultivates a more knowledgeable society.

Comprehending Media Appreciation

Media appreciation involves the competencies and understanding required to analyse, assess, and derive enjoyment from diverse media formats. It necessitates comprehension of the components that influence media production, encompassing the operational context, the techniques utilised, and the intended communications. By examining various media forms—such as film, television, print, music, and digital content—individuals can cultivate a more profound comprehension of their influence on culture and society.

THE FUNCTION OF MEDIA IN SOCIETY

Reflection on Culture

Media functions as a reflection of societal values, norms, and challenges. Media can depict varied experiences and viewpoints through films, television programs, music, and literature. Through the appreciation of media, audiences acquire insights into the cultures, identities, and social issues that influence their environment.

Influencing Public Discourse

The media significantly influences public opinion and discourse. News reports, documentaries, and opinion articles shape the perception and discourse surrounding issues. An analytical evaluation of media allows individuals to recognise bias, detect propaganda, and interact with various perspectives constructively.

Enabling Communication

Media serves as a medium for communication and connection, enabling individuals to exchange experiences, ideas, and narratives across distances. Valuing media prompts individuals to investigate how various communication modalities foster dialogue and comprehension among diverse audiences.

ELEMENTS OF MEDIA APPRECIATION

Aesthetic Comprehension

Media appreciation entails acknowledging and valuing the artistic components that enhance a media text's influence. This encompasses an understanding of cinematography, sound design, editing, narrative structure, and visual composition. Through the examination of these elements, audiences can acquire insights into the creator's artistic decisions and the emotional reactions elicited by the work.

Cultural Context

Each media artefact exists within a cultural and historical framework that affects its production and interpretation. Comprehending the social, political, and economic influences that govern media production enables audiences to recognise the importance of media texts beyond mere entertainment. This cultural context is essential for identifying the target audience and the wider dialogues that media participates in.

Critical Engagement

Media appreciation entails a critical examination of media texts, prompting audiences to interrogate, analyse, and deliberate the conveyed messages. This encompasses the examination of representation, power dynamics, and ethical considerations in media. Critical engagement cultivates an understanding of how media can either reinforce or contest societal norms and ideologies.

Individual Contemplation

Interacting with media ought to stimulate introspection. Individuals ought to reflect on how media aligns with their experiences, convictions, and sentiments. This reflective practice fosters a profound engagement with the media consumed and assists audiences in articulating their reactions and interpretations.

PRAGMATIC STRATEGIES FOR MEDIA APPRECIATION

Media Consumption Logs

Maintaining a media consumption journal can augment appreciation by prompting individuals to contemplate their viewing, reading, or listening experiences. In this journal, individuals may document their responses, examine themes, and reflect on the cultural context of each work. This practice fosters critical thinking and facilitates deeper engagement with media.

Analysis of Film and Literature

Conducting a systematic analysis of films, literature, or other media can enhance appreciation. This may involve analysing narrative structure, character development, and thematic elements. Discussions or written analyses can enhance a shared comprehension of how various elements interact to generate meaning.

Engaging in Workshops

Workshops centred on media creation—such as filmmaking, writing, or digital content production—enable individuals to comprehend the challenges and creative choices inherent in media production. Comprehending the production process enables audiences to cultivate a deeper appreciation for the intricacies of media texts.

Participating in Screenings and Discussions

Engaging in screenings accompanied by discussions or panels can yield significant insights into the creative process and societal ramifications of media texts. Interacting with filmmakers, critics, and scholars can deepen comprehension and appreciation by providing varied perspectives.

5 .Investigating Varied Media

Proactively exploring varied media, including international cinema, independent works, and under-represented narratives, can expand viewpoints and enhance appreciation. Interacting with diverse narratives cultivates empathy and comprehension, emphasising the complexity of human experiences.

OBSTACLES IN MEDIA APPRECIATION

Media Saturation

In a media-saturated world, individuals may feel inundated by the vast amount of information accessible. This excess may result in passive consumption instead of deliberate engagement. To address this, individuals should prioritise quality over quantity, choosing particular pieces for in-depth analysis and appreciation.

Disinformation and Prejudice

The prevalence of misinformation and biassed reporting presents obstacles to media appreciation. It is imperative for individuals to develop critical skills to evaluate credible sources and recognise biases. This analytical perspective allows audiences to interact thoughtfully with media while traversing intricate narratives.

Cultural Sensitivity

Media portrayals can reinforce stereotypes and marginalise specific groups. Critically engaging with media requires an understanding of cultural sensitivity and ethical considerations in representation. Media consumers ought to endeavour to value creations that confront stereotypes and advocate for inclusivity.

The Future of Media Appreciation

As technology advances, the media landscape will also transform. Virtual reality, augmented reality, and interactive media offer novel opportunities and challenges for appreciation. As audiences explore these new formats, the principles of media appreciation—critical engagement, aesthetic comprehension, cultural context, and personal reflection—will continue to be essential.

Furthermore, as media literacy is increasingly acknowledged as a vital competency, incorporating media appreciation into educational curricula can cultivate a more informed and engaged populace. By providing individuals with the means to critically evaluate and appreciate media, society can foster a culture of discerning media consumption and production.

The Significance of Media Appreciation

1.Cultural Understanding:
Media reflects cultural values, beliefs, and practices. Valuing various media formats enriches comprehension of distinct cultures and viewpoints.

2.Analytical Involvement:

Media appreciation promotes critical engagement with content, enhancing awareness of media's role in shaping public opinion and influencing societal norms.

3.Engaged Involvement:

By valuing media, individuals transform into informed consumers and producers, equipped to engage in discourse regarding media representation, ethics, and influence.

4.Innovation and Articulation:

Comprehending diverse media formats can stimulate creative expression and motivate individuals to investigate their own media production abilities.

Media Formats

1.Visual Media: Encompasses photography, film, and visual art, conveying messages through imagery and design.

2.Audio Media: Encompasses radio, podcasts, and music, captivating audiences through auditory experiences and narrative techniques.

3.Printed Media: Includes newspapers, magazines, and books, providing comprehensive analysis and narratives on diverse subjects.

4.Digital Media: Encompasses websites, blogs, and social media, facilitating interactive engagement and varied content creation.

5.Performing Arts: Integrates theatre, dance, and live performances, articulating narratives and emotions through physical expressions.

Pragmatic Endeavours to Augment Media Appreciation

1.Media Consumption Record:

Participants are required to document their media consumption over the course of one week, detailing the types of media engaged with, the messages communicated, and their personal reflections.

2.Critiques of Media:

Assign participants to compose reviews of various media forms (films, books, music albums) emphasising themes, cultural significance, and personal impact.

3.Media Workshops:

Facilitate workshops in which participants produce their own media content, examining diverse formats (e.g., short films, podcasts, visual art).

4.Media Excursions:

Arrange visits to local media institutions, art galleries, or theatres to familiarise participants with diverse media practices and viewpoints.

5.Discussion Panels:

Facilitate panels or discussions with media professionals, artists, and critics to examine the importance of media in society.

Internship

1.Invited Presentations:

Invite media scholars or industry experts to impart their experiences and insights regarding particular media forms and their societal impact.

2. Film Screenings:

Organize screenings of films or documentaries followed by discussions to analyse themes, techniques, and cultural significance.

3. Art Exhibitions:

Arrange visits to art exhibitions where participants can appreciate visual media and engage with artists about their work.

Critical Media Literacy

In today's fast-paced and information-rich world, the ability to critically engage with media is more important than ever. Critical media literacy (CML) is a framework that equips individuals with the skills necessary to analyse, evaluate, and create media messages thoughtfully and critically.

As media saturation continues to grow, CML empowers people to navigate the complexities of media landscapes, fostering informed and active citizenship.

The Importance of Critical Media Literacy

1. Empowerment Through Knowledge

Critical media literacy enables individuals to understand how media works and influences society. It empowers them to discern the motives behind media messages, recognize bias and propaganda, and make informed decisions about what to consume and share. In an era where misinformation is prevalent, CML equips individuals with the tools to sift through noise, identify credible sources, and engage meaningfully with content.

2. Fostering Critical Thinking

CML promotes critical thinking skills, encouraging individuals to question and analyse media rather than passively accept it. By examining the messages conveyed through various media forms—news articles, advertisements, social media posts, films, and more—individuals can develop a deeper understanding of the underlying ideologies, values, and social constructs. This critical engagement enhances their ability to form independent opinions and challenge dominant narratives.

3. Understanding Representation and Identity

Media has a powerful role in shaping perceptions of identity, culture, and society. Critical media literacy allows individuals to explore how different groups are represented in media and the implications of these representations. By analysing portrayals of race, gender, class, and sexuality, individuals can understand how media influences societal norms and attitudes. This awareness can lead to greater empathy and social responsibility.

4. Promoting Active Citizenship

Informed citizens are better equipped to participate in democratic processes. CML fosters civic engagement by encouraging individuals to critically assess media messages related to political issues, public policy, and social justice. By understanding the role of media in shaping public discourse, individuals can engage in meaningful discussions, advocate for change, and hold media organizations accountable for their practices.

Key Components of Critical Media Literacy

Access

The first component of CML involves the ability to access diverse media sources. This includes understanding how to navigate different platforms, whether traditional (e.g., newspapers, television) or digital (e.g., social media, websites). Access also entails recognizing biases in information sources and understanding how algorithms shape what content is seen.

Analysis

Critical analysis is fundamental to CML. This entails analysing media content for its messages, methodologies, and foundational ideologies. Individuals acquire the ability to discern narrative frameworks, visual storytelling methodologies, and persuasive tactics employed in advertising and news dissemination. Through the examination of media's construction of meaning, individuals can gain insight into the underlying intentions of content and its potential effects on audiences.

Assessment

Assessing media entails evaluating the reliability of sources and identifying biases that may influence the depiction of information. Individuals acquire the ability to differentiate between opinion and fact, comprehend the ramifications of sensationalism, and assess the credibility of information disseminated in media. This skill is crucial for countering misinformation and making informed choices regarding what to trust and disseminate.

Formation

The capacity to produce media is a fundamental component of CML. Individuals are urged to create their own media content, be it through writing, video production, or digital art. This process entails comprehending the ethical ramifications of media production, including representation, accuracy, and the possible effects on audiences. Through media creation, individuals can articulate their viewpoints, contest prevailing narratives, and enhance public discourse.

Practical Activities for Developing Critical Media Literacy

1. Media Consumption Diary

Participants maintain a diary documenting their media consumption over a week. They note the types of media accessed, the messages conveyed, and their personal reactions. This reflective exercise encourages individuals to become more conscious of their media habits and the impact of media on their thoughts and behaviours.

2. Media Analysis Exercises

Assign participants to analyse specific media pieces, such as advertisements, news articles, or films. They should identify the target audience, key messages, and any biases present. This activity helps participants practice critical thinking and analytical skills while fostering discussions around representation and ideology.

3. Debate and Discussion Forums

Organize discussions around current media topics, such as the role of social media in shaping public opinion or the ethics of media representation. Encourage participants to use evidence and analysis to support their viewpoints, fostering a collaborative learning environment.

4.Verification Workshops

Instruct participants on the methodology of fact-checking by scrutinising sources and corroborating assertions. This workshop may encompass discussions on credible resources, the significance of scepticism, and the competencies required to discern misinformation.

5.Innovative Counter-Narratives

Participants produce media artefacts, including videos or articles, that contest prevailing narratives or stereotypes. This exercise fosters creativity and enables individuals to express their viewpoints while emphasising the significance of representation in media.

Fostering a Critical Media Literacy Perspective

1.Foster Inquiry

Encourage a mindset of inquiry by prompting participants to question the media they engage with. What is the objective of this communication? Who was the producer? What values are being conveyed? This inquisitive disposition fosters curiosity and analytical reasoning.

2.Encourage Varied Viewpoints

Engagement with varied viewpoints is essential for cultivating critical media literacy. Urge participants to explore media from diverse cultures, perspectives, and backgrounds. This practice fosters comprehension and appreciation of diversity while confronting stereotypes.

3.Participate in Contemporary Affairs

Motivate participants to remain knowledgeable about contemporary events and critically assess the media's portrayal of them. This engagement enables individuals to correlate theory with practical issues, thereby underscoring the significance of CML in comprehending societal dynamics.

4.Promote Media Literacy Education

Advocate for the significance of media literacy education within educational institutions and communities. Promote curricula that incorporate CML principles, guaranteeing that future generations possess the skills required to adeptly navigate the media landscape.

Media Appreciation: Comprehending and Interacting with Media

In an era where media permeates all facets of our existence, from the news we engage with to the entertainment we enjoy, cultivating a sophisticated understanding of media is imperative. Media appreciation entails active engagement with media content, considering its aesthetic, cultural, and social implications rather than mere passive consumption.

This thorough comprehension promotes critical analysis, improves personal articulation, and cultivates a more enlightened society.

Comprehending Media Appreciation

Media appreciation involves the competencies and understanding required to analyse, assess, and derive enjoyment from diverse media formats. It necessitates comprehension of the components that influence media production, encompassing the operational context, the employed techniques, and the intended messages. By examining various media forms—such as film, television, print, music, and digital content—individuals can cultivate a more profound comprehension of their influence on culture and society.

The Function of Media in Society

1.Reflection on Culture

Media functions as a reflection of societal values, norms, and challenges. Media can depict varied experiences and viewpoints through films, television programs, music, and literature. Through the appreciation of media, audiences acquire insights into the cultures, identities, and social issues that influence their environment.

2.Influencing Public Discourse

The media significantly influences public opinion and discourse. News reports, documentaries, and opinion articles shape the perception and discourse surrounding issues. An analytical evaluation of media empowers individuals to recognise bias, detect propaganda, and interact with varied perspectives constructively.

3.Enabling Communication

Media serves as a medium for communication and connection, enabling individuals to exchange experiences, ideas, and narratives across distances. Valuing media prompts individuals to investigate how various communication modalities foster dialogue and comprehension among diverse audiences.

Elements of Media Appreciation

1.Aesthetic Understanding

Media appreciation entails acknowledging and valuing the artistic components that enhance a media text's influence. This encompasses knowledge of cinematography, sound design, editing, narrative structure, and visual composition. Through the analysis of these elements, audiences can acquire insights into the creator's artistic decisions and the emotional reactions elicited by the work.

2.Cultural Context

Each media artefact exists within a cultural and historical framework that affects its production and reception. Comprehending the social, political, and economic influences that govern media production enables audiences to recognise the importance of media texts beyond mere entertainment. The cultural context is essential for identifying the target audience and the wider dialogues that media participates in.

3.Critical Engagement

Media appreciation entails a critical engagement with media texts, prompting audiences to interrogate, analyse, and deliberate the conveyed messages. This encompasses the examination of representation, power dynamics, and ethics in media. Critical engagement cultivates an understanding of how media can either reinforce or contest societal norms and ideologies.

4.Individual Contemplation

Interaction with media should stimulate introspection. Individuals ought to reflect on how media aligns with their experiences, convictions, and emotions. This reflective practice fosters a profound connection to the media consumed and assists audiences in articulating their responses and interpretations.

Pragmatic Strategies for Media Appreciation

1.Media Consumption Logs

Maintaining a media consumption journal can augment appreciation by prompting individuals to contemplate their viewing, reading, or listening experiences. This journal allows individuals to document their responses, examine themes, and reflect on the cultural context of each work. This practice fosters critical thinking and facilitates deeper engagement with media.

2.Analysis of Film and Literature

Conducting a systematic analysis of films, literature, or other media can enhance appreciation. This may involve analysing narrative structure, character development, and thematic elements. Discussions or written analyses can enhance a shared comprehension of how various elements colLabourate to generate meaning.

3.Engaging in Workshop

Workshops centred on media creation—encompassing filmmaking, writing, or digital content production—enable individuals to comprehend the challenges and creative choices inherent in media production. Comprehending the production process enables audiences to cultivate a deeper appreciation for the intricacies of media texts.

4.Participating in Screenings and Discussions

Engaging in screenings accompanied by discussions or panels can yield significant insights into the creative process and societal ramifications of media texts. Interacting with filmmakers, critics, and scholars can enrich comprehension and appreciation by providing varied viewpoints.

5.Investigating Varied Media

Proactively exploring varied media, including international cinema, independent works, and under-represented narratives, can expand viewpoints and enhance appreciation. Engaging with varied narratives fosters empathy and understanding, highlighting the richness of human experiences.

Challenges in Media Appreciation

1. Media Overload

In a world saturated with media content, individuals may feel overwhelmed by the sheer volume of information available. This overload can lead to passive consumption rather than thoughtful engagement. To combat this, individuals should focus on quality over quantity, selecting specific pieces to analyse and appreciate deeply.

2. Misinformation and Bias

The prevalence of misinformation and biased reporting poses challenges for media appreciation. It becomes essential for individuals to cultivate critical skills to discern credible sources and identify biases. This critical lens enables audiences to engage thoughtfully with media while navigating complex narratives.

3. Cultural Sensitivity

Media representations can perpetuate stereotypes and marginalize certain groups. Critically engaging with media requires an understanding of cultural sensitivity and ethical considerations in representation. Media consumers ought to endeavour to value creations that confront stereotypes and advocate for inclusivity.

The Future of Media Appreciation

As technology advances, the media landscape will also transform. Virtual reality, augmented reality, and interactive media offer novel opportunities and challenges for appreciation. As audiences explore these new formats, the principles of media appreciation—critical engagement, aesthetic comprehension, cultural context, and personal reflection—will continue to be essential.

Furthermore, as media literacy is increasingly acknowledged as a vital competency, incorporating media appreciation into educational curricula can cultivate a more informed and engaged populace. By providing individuals with the means to critically evaluate and appreciate media, society can foster a culture of discerning media consumption and production.

CREATION OF MEDIA CONTENT

Comprehending Media Content Production

In the digital era, media content creation has become a fundamental aspect of daily existence. Individuals and organisations are increasingly involved in the creation and distribution of media content, ranging from social media posts and YouTube videos to podcasts and blog articles. This phenomenon reflects both technological advancements and the evolving dynamics of communication in modern society. Media content creation involves various activities focused on generating and disseminating information, entertainment, and artistic expression. Analysing this process from a sociological perspective enables an examination of its ramifications for society, culture, and personal identity.

The Sociocultural Framework of Media Production

The creation of media content is shaped by diverse sociocultural factors, such as social norms, power dynamics, and cultural contexts. Individuals produce and disseminate media within a context influenced by their social surroundings, identities, and values. The sociological perspective highlights that media functions not only as a communication tool but also as a social process capable of reinforcing or contesting societal norms.

Societal Norms and Expectations

Social norms govern the permissible methods by which individuals may articulate themselves via media. These norms may differ significantly due to factors including age, gender, ethnicity, and social class. The content that receives acclaim or censure frequently mirrors overarching societal values and expectations.

In numerous societies, there exist normative expectations regarding what is deemed "appropriate" content for particular platforms. Instagram, prioritising aesthetics, may incentivise users to share visually captivating images, whereas Twitter's character restriction fosters conciseness and promptness. Platform-specific conventions influence content creation and reception, frequently compelling creators to adhere to established styles and trends.

Power Dynamics in Media Creation

The sociological lens also sheds light on the power dynamics inherent in media content creation. Traditional media has historically been dominated by a few major corporations and gatekeepers who controlled the flow of information. However, the rise of digital platforms has democratized media production, allowing individuals to become content creators in their own right.

This shift has both positive and negative implications. On one hand, it empowers marginalized voices and provides a platform for diverse perspectives. On the other hand, it can lead to the perpetuation of misinformation and the proliferation of harmful content. Understanding these power dynamics is crucial for creators as they navigate the media landscape and seek to make their voices heard.

The Process of Media Content Creation

Media content creation involves several stages, from conceptualization to distribution. Each phase is shaped by social influences, technological tools, and individual creativity.

Conceptualization and Ideation

The first step in media content creation is conceptualization, where the creator develops an idea for their content. This phase is often influenced by personal interests, current trends, and audience expectations. A content creator may derive inspiration from social issues, popular culture, or personal experiences, thereby reflecting their identity and values.

This stage is significant sociologically as it underscores the manner in which creators interact with their social milieu. The concepts they select for examination are frequently influenced by the dominant cultural narratives and discourses in society. The interplay between personal creativity and societal influences determines the themes and messages of the produced content.

Manufacturing

Upon the solidification of the concept, the production phase commences. This entails the production of media content, including video filming, podcast recording, article writing, or graphic design. At this stage, creators utilise diverse tools and technologies to actualise their concepts. Production is not solely a technical procedure; it is also a cooperative endeavour. Numerous creators engage in collaborative efforts, either through informal alliances or formal partnerships. This collaborative element underscores the significance of community and social networks in media production, where skills and resources are exchanged to improve the quality of the generated content.

Dissemination and Allocation

Upon creation, the content must be disseminated to reach its target audience. The emergence of social media and online platforms has revolutionised the distribution process, enabling creators to disseminate their work broadly and instantaneously. This accessibility has facilitated the emergence of new audiences and communities, allowing creators to engage with individuals who possess shared interests and values.

Nonetheless, distribution also prompts enquiries regarding visibility and acknowledgement. Digital platforms offer exposure opportunities but also establish a competitive environment where creators must manage algorithms, audience interaction, and content marketing. Comprehending the intricacies of distribution is essential for creators aiming to enhance their messages and expand their audiences.

The Influence of Audience in Media Content Development

The relationship between creators and audiences is a dynamic and interactive process that influences media content. Audience engagement manifests in multiple ways, such as feedback, sharing, and involvement in content creation. This interaction is especially evident in the digital era, where audiences can directly engage with creators and impact the content being generated.

Audience Evaluation

Historically, audience feedback was predominantly restricted to formal critiques or evaluations. Contemporary digital platforms facilitate instantaneous feedback, permitting creators to address comments, critiques, and suggestions from their audiences. This direct engagement can guide subsequent content choices, as creators modify their work to correspond with audience inclinations.

From a sociological standpoint, audience feedback signifies the dynamic character of communication within a participatory culture. Audiences have transitioned from passive consumers to active participants, influencing the media content they experience. This participatory model cultivates a sense of community and connection between creators and their audiences.

Cooperative Development

Alongside feedback, numerous creators encourage their audiences to engage in the content creation process. This collaborative method can manifest in several ways, including crowd-sourced projects, fan art, or community-driven initiatives. By engaging audiences in the creative process, creators can cultivate stronger connections and instill a sense of ownership among their followers.

Collaboration challenges conventional concepts of authorship and ownership in media production. It obscures the distinction between creator and audience, emphasising the collaborative essence of media production in the digital era. This sociological transformation signifies wider alterations in our comprehension of creativity and societal contribution.

The Significance of Critical Media Literacy

1.Empowerment:

Through the cultivation of critical media literacy, individuals are empowered as discerning consumers of media. They acquire the capacity to interrogate, evaluate, and interact with media messages, instead of passively accepting them.

2.Knowledgeable Citizenship:

Critical media literacy promotes informed participation in democratic processes. It empowers individuals to identify bias, propaganda, and misinformation, thereby fostering active engagement in civic life.

3.Cultural Awareness:

Comprehending media narratives enables individuals to value cultural diversity and discern how media can either perpetuate or contest stereotypes and social norms.

4.Resistance to Misinformation:

In an age of widespread misinformation, critical media literacy provides individuals with the skills to identify credible sources, promoting a more informed populace.

Essential Elements of Critical Media Literacy

1.Access:

The capacity to identify and retrieve various media sources, encompassing traditional, digital, and social media.

2.Examination:

The ability to critically analyse media content, recognising the techniques employed to shape audience perceptions, the values depicted, and the socio-political context.

3.Assessment:

The ability to evaluate the reliability of information sources, differentiate between fact and opinion, and identify potential biases.

4.Formation:

The capacity to generate media content that conveys messages efficiently while conforming to ethical principles and fostering social consciousness.

Essential Competencies of Critical Media Literacy

1. Access: The capacity to identify and obtain diverse media sources, encompassing both traditional and digital platforms.

2. Analysis: The ability to critically evaluate media content, identifying the implicit messages, biases, and methods employed to construct narratives.

3. Assessment: The capacity to appraise the credibility and reliability of sources, differentiate between fact and opinion, and recognise potential biases.

4. Creation: The skill to create media content that communicates messages effectively, using appropriate formats and techniques to engage the audience.

Practical Activities to Develop Critical Media Literacy

1. Media Journals:

Participants maintain a media journal, documenting their media consumption, reflecting on the content, and analysing the messages conveyed.
Prompts: Include questions like "What messages are being communicated?", "Who is the intended audience?", and "What biases might exist?".

2. Media Analysis Assignments:

Assign participants to select a specific media piece (e.g., an article, advertisement, or film) and conduct a thorough analysis.
Guidelines: Analyse elements such as language, imagery, target audience, and the broader social context in which the media exists.

3. Debate and Discussion:

Organize debates on current media topics (e.g., censorship, representation in media, the impact of social media).

Encourage participants to use evidence and analysis to support their positions, fostering critical thinking and discussion skills.

4. Develop Counter-narratives:

Participants will produce media content (e.g., videos, articles) that contest prevailing narratives or stereotypes found in mainstream media.

Encourage the emphasis on under-represented voices or alternative perspectives.

5.Verification Initiatives:

Facilitate workshops on fact-checking methodologies, instructing participants on how to assess the credibility of information sources.

Utilise contemporary instances of misinformation to hone the skill of recognising false assertions.

Practicum

1.Workshops on Media Instruments:

Conduct workshops on media analysis tools (e.g., MediaSmarts, FactCheck.org) to equip participants with resources for assessing media content.

2.Invited Speakers:

Invite journalists, media analysts, or educators with expertise in media literacy to convey their insights and experiences.

3 .Excursions:

Facilitate visits to media organisations, allowing participants to observe the media production process and interact with industry professionals.

Pragmatic Exercises for Cultivating Critical Media Literacy

1.Media Consumption Log:

Participants maintain a diary documenting their media consumption, specifying the types of media accessed, the messages communicated, and their individual responses. This reflection promotes consciousness of media consumption patterns.

2 .Exercises in Media Analysis:

Designate participants to examine particular media artefacts (e.g., an advertisement, news article, or film). They must ascertain the target audience, principal messages, and any inherent biases.

3.Forums for Debate and Discussion:

Facilitate dialogues concerning contemporary media issues (e.g., the influence of social media on public perception, matters of representation). Encourage participants to use evidence and analysis to support their viewpoints.

4. Fact-Checking Workshops:
Teach participants how to fact-check information, emphasizing the importance of verifying sources and identifying misinformation.

5. Creative Counter-narratives:

Participants create media pieces (e.g., videos, articles) that challenge dominant narratives or stereotypes, promoting diverse perspectives and social justice.

Practicum

1. Guest Speakers:

Invite media professionals, educators, or activists to share their experiences with media literacy and its impact on society.

2. Field Trips:

Organize visits to media organizations, where participants can observe media production processes and engage with professionals about ethical practices.

3. Joint Initiatives:

Promote group projects aimed at analysing and critiquing local media, thereby enhancing teamwork and collaborative critical thinking.

Fostering critical media literacy is imperative in the contemporary information-centric society. By cultivating competencies in access, analysis, evaluation, and creation, individuals can interact with media more thoughtfully and critically. These skills enable individuals to traverse the media landscape, engage actively in society, and foster a more informed populace.

———

Bibliography

Althusser, L. (1971). *Ideology and Ideological State Apparatuses. In Lenin and Philosophy and Other Essays* (pp. 127-186). New Left Books.

Anderson, B. (1983). *Imagined Communities: Reflections on the Origin and Spread of Nationalism.* Verso.

Bauman, Z. (2000). *Liquid Modernity.* Polity Press.

Baudrillard, J. (1981). *Simulacra and Simulation.* University of Michigan Press.

Benjamin, W. (1968). *The Work of Art in the Age of Mechanical Reproduction. In Illuminations* (pp. 217-251). Schocken Books.

Bourdieu, P. (1977). *Outline of a Theory of Practice.* Cambridge University Press.

Castells, M. (1996). *The Rise of the Network Society.* Blackwell Publishers.

Couldry, N. (2012). *Media, Society, World: Social Theory and Digital Media Practice.* Polity Press.

Dayan, D., & Katz, E. (1992). *Media Events: The Live Broadcasting of History.* Harvard University Press.

De Saussure, F. (1916). *Course in General Linguistics.* McGraw-Hill.

Foucault, M. (1972). *The Archaeology of Knowledge.* Pantheon Books.

Gramsci, A. (1971). *Selections from the Prison Notebooks.* International Publishers.

Habermas, J. (1989). *The Structural Transformation of the Public Sphere.* MIT Press.

Hall, S. (1980). *Encoding/Decoding. In Culture, Media, Language* (pp. 128-138). Hutchinson.

Horkheimer, M., & Adorno, T. W. (2002). The Culture Industry: Enlightenment as Mass Deception. *In Dialectic of Enlightenment: Philosophical Fragments.* Stanford University Press.

Innis, H. A. (1951). *The Bias of Communication.* University of Toronto Press.

Jenkins, H. (2006). *Convergence Culture: Where Old and New Media Collide.* New York University Press.

Katz, E., & Lazarsfeld, P. F. (1955). *Personal Influence: The Part Played by People in the Flow of Mass Communications.* Free Press.

McLuhan, M. (1964). *Understanding Media: The Extensions of Man.* McGraw-Hill.

Mulvey, L. (1975). Visual Pleasure and Narrative Cinema. *Screen,* 16(3), 6-18.

Ong, W. J. (1982). *Orality and Literacy: The Technologizing of the Word.* Methuen.

Williams, R. (1974). *Television: Technology and Cultural Form.* Fontana.